The French-Speaking World

'This workbook assumes virtually no prior knowledge of linguistics/sociolinguistics and presents a range of lively and up-to-date material in an accessible way.'
Carol Sanders, *Department of Linguistic and International Studies, University of Surrey*

This accessible textbook offers students the opportunity to explore for themselves a wide range of sociolinguistic issues relating to the French language and its role in societies around the world. It is written for undergraduate students who have a sound practical knowledge of French but who have little or no knowledge of linguistics or sociolinguistics. It combines text with practical exercises and discussion questions to stimulate readers to think for themselves and to tackle specific problems.

In **Part one** Rodney Ball looks at the diversity of the French-speaking world and the function of French in particular countries and regions, including Belgium, Canada and Switzerland. He explores its status in relation to other languages and its role in inter-community relations. In **Part two** the focus shifts to individual language features, and among topics explored are regional speech forms, the differences between written and spoken French, the 'social meaning' of different styles and levels of language, and the use of French by immigrants. **Part three** looks at recent developments and controversies affecting the French language, particularly in France itself.

Key features of this book:

- **Informative and comprehensive:** covers a wide range of current issues
- **Practical:** contains a variety of graded exercises and tasks plus an index of terms
- **Topical and contemporary:** deals with current situations and provides up-to-date illustrative material
- **Thought-provoking:** encourages students to reflect and research for themselves

Rodney Ball is a lecturer in French in the School of Modern Languages at Southampton University. He teaches general linguistics and French sociolinguistics, on which he has published a number of articles, and is involved in designing practical language courses.

Routledge Language in Society

The **Routledge Language in Society** series provides the basis for a typical one-semester course. It combines a review of current sociolinguistic themes and relevant reading with a range of practical tasks exploring particular topics, and a selection of readings illustrating the socio-political significance of language-related issues. The focus encourages students to engage directly with important linguistic issues in a variety of ways. The outcome of this process is that students have a greater knowledge of, and sensitivity to, sociolinguistic problems and are able to observe and explore these problems when they have the opportunity to experience them at first hand.

EXISTING TITLES:

The French-Speaking World
Rodney Ball, *School of Modern Languages,*
University of Southampton

The German-Speaking World
Patrick Stevenson, *School of Modern Languages,*
University of Southampton

The Spanish-Speaking World
Clare Mar-Molinero, *School of Modern Languages,*
University of Southampton

LONDON AND NEW YORK

The French-Speaking World

A practical introduction to sociolinguistic issues

• Rodney Ball

First published 1997
by Routledge
11 New Fetter Lane, London EC4P 4EE

Simultaneously published in the USA and
Canada
by Routledge
29 West 35th Street, New York, NY10001

Typeset in Sabon, Futura, Times and Optima
by Keystroke, Jacaranda Lodge,
Wolverhampton
Printed and bound in Great Britain by
TJ International Ltd, Padstow, Cornwall

*British Library Cataloguing in Publication
Data*
A catalogue record for this book is available
from the British Library

*Library of Congress Cataloguing in
Publication Data*
Ball, Rodney, 1940–
   The French-Speaking world : a practical
introduction to sociolinguistic issues /
Rodney Ball.
      (Routledge language in society : 1)
      Includes bibliographical references and
index.
      1. French language—Social aspects—
Foreign countries.
      2. French language—
Social aspects—France.
      3. Sociolinguistics.
I. Title. II. Series.
PC2074.75.B35 1997
306.4'444—dc20   96–43951

ISBN 0–415–12986–9 (hbk)
ISBN 0–415–12987–7 (pbk)

Contents

Part three

INNOVATION, CONSERVATION AND DEFENCE

11 Official innovation: the role of the State 187

12 Defending and preserving the language 205

Maps

Acknowledgements

The author wishes to express his appreciation for the support and encouragement received from his fellow contributors to this series, Clare Mar-Molinero and Patrick Stevenson.

The author and publisher gratefully acknowledge permission from the following to quote from copyright material: Böhlau Verlag, Champion-Slatkine, Éditions Albin Michel, Éditions Denoël, Éditions Fleuve Noir, Éditions Hors Collection, Éditions Klincksieck, Éditions Payot, Éditions Reclus, Éditions La Découverte, *L'Express, Langage et Société, Le Nouvel Observateur, Le Monde*, Librairie Plon, *Lire*, Mouton de Gruyter, Multilingual Matters Ltd, Nathan, the *New York Times* Syndication Sales Corporation, Publications de l'Université de Provence, Stanford University Press, Philippe Blanchet, Mathilde Fischer, Vivienne Mela, Raymond Mougeon, Ndiassé Thiam. Extracts from J. de la Guérivère, *Belgique: la revanche des langues*: Copyright © Éditions du Seuil, 1994. Extracts from P. Merle, *Dictionnaire du français branché suivi du guide du français tic et toc* and *Le Déchiros*: Copyright © Éditions du Seuil 1989, 1991 respectively. The extract from B. Seguin and F. Teillard, *Les Céfrans parlent aux Français*: Copyright © Calmann-Lévy, 1996. The extract from M. Richler, *Oh, Canada! Oh Quebec! Requiem for a Divided Country*: Copyright © Mordecai Richler Productions Inc. 1992. Reproduced by permission of the author c/o Rogers, Coleridge & White Ltd, London. The extract from M. Danner, 'Haiti on the Verge': Copyright

ACKNOWLEDGEMENTS

© 1993 Nyrev Inc. Reprinted with permission from the *New York Review of Books*. The extract from P. Gardner-Chloros, *Language Selection and Switching in Strasbourg*, 1991, is reproduced by permission of Oxford University Press. Details of other sources are supplied in the Bibliography.

Every effort has been made to contact copyright holders, although this has not been possible in all cases. Any omissions brought to our attention will be remedied in future editions.

Introduction

T HE AIM OF THIS BOOK is to offer students the opportunity to explore for themselves a wide range of sociolinguistic issues relating to the French language. It is intended principally for undergraduate students of French who have a reasonably advanced knowledge of the language, but who may have little or no knowledge of linguistics in general or sociolinguistics in particular. Relevant theoretical concepts are introduced where necessary, but the emphasis throughout is on encouraging readers to think for themselves and to tackle specific problems. To this end, each chapter is punctuated with a series of practical tasks and discussion questions designed to stimulate readers to pursue in greater depth issues raised in the text. Tasks include small-scale activities – working on definitions of concepts, commenting on accounts of particular linguistic situations or interpreting data presented in tabular form – and more wide-ranging reflective exercises – essays, projects, etc.

The book has been written with a typical semester-length course in mind, and it could therefore be worked through as the principal course text. However, although there is a progression within each chapter and through the three parts, it is hoped that the structure of the book is sufficiently flexible to allow it to be used in various ways to suit particular needs. For example, individual parts or chapters could be selected to complement other material, and students or tutors can decide for themselves which tasks to attempt. The tasks are graded in terms of difficulty and time required to tackle them: see 'How to use this book' below.

Part one initially considers the diversity of the 'French-speaking world', raising questions about the validity of this concept. It then focuses more specifically on certain selected countries or regions: readers are invited to investigate and reflect on fundamental 'macro-sociolinguistic' issues concerning the function of the French language within a given society, its status relative to other languages with which it is in contact and its role in inter-community relationships.

Part two aims to encourage readers to explore social and regional variation in French from a 'micro-sociolinguistic' perspective, shifting attention to individual language features, their functions and their significance for speakers. This involves, for example, considering regional speech forms, analysing differences between written and spoken French, investigating the 'social meaning' of different styles and levels of language, or examining the varieties of French used by immigrants. In addition, a link with the previous section is provided by the inclusion of a chapter on the French-based Creoles and their speakers.

Part three focuses on recent developments in the French language and on reactions towards them, particularly in France itself. Exercises illustrating aspects of innovation in vocabulary or grammar are intermingled with analysis of material that sheds light on opinions or attitudes (press excerpts, opinion surveys, etc.). Consideration is given to the fascination and concern generated by current trends, to the prominent role which the State seeks to play in modelling the future of the language, and to the widespread public debates about linguistic matters that have characterized recent years. Hand in hand with this goes an exploration of the conservative tradition of 'defence of the language'.

How to use this book

The tasks and discussion questions are intended to encourage readers to pause and reflect on issues as they go along and to give them the opportunity to pursue particular topics in greater depth. However, it is not necessary to attempt all the activities in order to follow the text.

It is assumed that readers will have access to an academic library and many of the tasks can be tackled only by making use of the resources normally found there. Readers will get most out of the book if they actively seek information and ideas from a wide as possible a range of other sources (e.g. newspapers, television and radio, the Internet). A few of the tasks presuppose contact with native speakers of French, and one or two may best be tackled during a period of residence in a French-speaking country. To help readers decide which tasks to attempt, they have been graded in terms of difficulty and/or the time and resources required:

■ a question or task that reinforces specific points in the text, in an excerpt or in a table, inviting the reader to give a quick reaction, a simple explanation or further factual information;

■■ a question or task relating to a broader issue and requiring reflection in greater depth, a more analytical explanation or a considered personal opinion;

■■■ a question or task that gives the reader an opportunity to undertake an extensive study going beyond what is actually covered in the text – for example, in the form of an essay, an empirical project or a discussion document. Such tasks normally involve further reading or independent investigation.

One or two general '■ ■ ■-type' tasks are provided at the end of each chapter (in addition to any others proposed in the course of it). This is to encourage the reader to follow up issues raised by the chapter as a whole.

Also included at the end of each chapter are 'Further reading' sections. Completion of many of the exercises will be greatly facilitated by following up the references provided. Only author and publication date are given: other details are to be found in the Bibliography.

Note, finally, that this book is not intended as an introduction to sociolinguistics as such. Where specialized terms and concepts are used that might be new to readers, they are briefly explained or illustrated, and listed at the end of the volume. More information about them, and of course about other general sociolinguistic topics, will be found in the following.

Reference works

Crystal, D. *The Cambridge Encyclopedia of Language*, Cambridge, Cambridge University Press, 1987.
—— *An Encyclopedic Dictionary of Language and Languages*, Oxford, Blackwell, 1992.

Introductory textbooks on general sociolinguistics

Fasold, R. *The Sociolinguistics of Society*, Oxford, Blackwell, 1984.
—— *The Sociolinguistics of Language*, Oxford, Blackwell, 1990.
Holmes, J. *An Introduction to Sociolinguistics*, London, Longman, 1992.
Wardhaugh, R. *An Introduction to Sociolinguistics*, Oxford, Blackwell, 1992.

• • •

The position
of French
in the world

Chapter 1

Le Monde francophone

Is French a 'world language'?

Here is some information about eight languages:

TABLE 1.1

Language	Native speakers (millions)	Official status in how many countries?	Significant presence on how many continents?	Official or working language of UN?
Chinese	1000	3	1	official
English	350	50	5	official and working
French	70	28	4	official and working
German	100	6	1	neither
Japanese	120	1	1	neither
Portuguese	135	7	2	neither
Russian	150	1	2	official
Spanish	280	20	2	official

Sources: Comrie 1987 (col. 2), Crystal 1987 (col. 2)

■ Specify some of the countries referred to in column 2.

■ Specify the continents in question in column 3, saying which of the countries are found in which continent.

The languages in Table 1.1 obviously differ greatly in respect of the various parameters. Japanese, for instance, is a 'major language' in the sense that it has a large number of native speakers, and Japan is a world power economically. However, outside Japan itself, the language has no official status and few speakers (other than expatriates). For these reasons, it is unlikely to qualify as a 'world' or 'international' language. English, by contrast, could hardly be denied such a status, given the number of countries where it is used.

■■ Though it has the smallest number of native speakers, French comes second only to English in terms of the number of countries where it is official. Why is this, do you think?

■■ Compare French with the other languages and see whether you can draw up a 'league table', in which, presumably, English would come first in terms of overall world importance. Say what criteria you are taking into account, and whether they conflict with one another.

In lists of the world's 'twelve major languages', Arabic, Bengali, Hindustani and Malay are often included as well as the eight in the table. However, Italian, Swahili or Turkish would be unlikely to figure in it.

■   Obtain basic data for these languages.

■■ Then justify their presence (or absence) in lists of the 'top twelve'.

One important factor not included in the table (because even approximate figures are hard to obtain) is the extent to which the various languages are learnt by people who aren't native speakers of them. (See below for estimates of the number of 'second-language speakers' of French.)

■■ How do you think French would compare with the other languages in this respect?

■■ Does this affect its position on your league table?

Many people have tried to assess the importance of French. The following are among the characterizations that have been made in recent years:

> Le français . . . est, avec l'anglais, la langue la plus importante du monde.
>
> (Muller 1985: 9)

> . . . la deuxième langue de grande diffusion après l'anglais.
>
> (Léger 1987: 2)

■■ Are such descriptions justified by the facts?

■■■ Is it possible to give clear and useful definitions of expressions like 'world language', 'international language' or 'major language'?

Most of the languages in the table owe their current status and distribution to fairly recent expansionism of one kind or another. Russian and Chinese have expanded overland; English, French, Portuguese and Spanish originated in countries which subsequently acquired extensive possessions overseas.

■■ Compare these last four languages in respect of the relative prominence (population, economic strength, political importance) of the 'mother' country among the countries where the language is used today. What is distinctive about the position of French?

The status of French in Europe differs in various ways from its status in the wider world. Table 1.2 gives some information about the official languages of the EU. (Note that, in actual day-to-day practice, English and French are the working languages of the EU administration.)

TABLE 1.2

Language	Native speakers in Europe (millions)	Number of European countries where it has official status	EU school pupils studying it as a foreign language (millions)
Danish	5.1	1	<0.1
Dutch	23.1	2	0.2
English	61.4	2	18.1
Finnish	5.1	1	<0.1
French	67.1	5	9.1
German	90.3	6	2.9
Greek	10.1	1	<0.1
Italian	57.7	3	0.2
Portuguese	10.4	1	0.1
Spanish	39.1	1	1.3
Swedish	9.1	1	<0.1

Sources: Rossillon 1995 (col. 2), Stevenson 1995 (col. 4)

■ Specify the countries referred to in column 3.

■■ Make some comparisons between the status and use of French and that of other European languages within Europe and worldwide.

At the height of the Napoleonic period, at a time when France was the most populous and powerful country in Europe, and its culture the continent's most prestigious, a French printer and amateur grammarian made the following observation about the language and its prospects:

> La langue française se propage de jour en jour avec tant de rapidité, que l'on peut espérer de la voir bientôt universellement adoptée en Europe.
>
> (D'Hautel 1808)

■■■ What subsequent factors and events made this an inaccurate prediction?

L'Espace francophone

Francophone ('French-speaking') can be used either as an adjective (*un pays francophone, le monde francophone*) or as a noun (*cinquante millions de francophones*). Uses like *un journal francophone* ('French-language newspaper') are quite common, though frowned upon by sticklers for accuracy (on the grounds that newspapers can't speak).

■ What language is spoken by each of the following groups?

anglophones, germanophones, hispanophones, lusophones, néerlandophones.

The centre of *le monde francophone* (known more grandly as *l'espace francophone*) is of course *la France métropolitaine*. This comprises mainland France plus offshore islands administered as part of a mainland department (e.g. the Ile de Ré), and also Corsica, which consists of two departments in its own right. Not included in the definition are the distant *départements et territoires d'outre-mer – les DOM-TOM –* which are nevertheless integral parts of the Republic (see Chapter 3 for the difference between them).

■ Identify the four DOM and the four TOM. Also the two further overseas dependencies with the intermediate status of *collectivités territoriales*.

■ Which of the ten is inhabited only by scientific research workers?

For reasons that should be obvious, it is often convenient and always fashionable to refer to mainland France as *l'Hexagone* (conventional term: *la France continentale*).

■ Draw a six-sided map of France, and then translate into (fashionable) French: 'There are fifty-six million French-speakers in France.'

From *francophone* comes the noun *francophonie* (it was coined as long ago as 1880). This looks as though it should mean 'the fact of being a French-speaker' (cf. *francophile/francophilie*). However, it's often not used in this way, referring instead either to 'l'ensemble des pays de langue française' (over forty of them worldwide), or else to the network of organizations linking them.

Table 1.3 provides more detail about the sixteen most populous francophone (or partly francophone) countries (see also Map 1.1). In each case, French has one or more of the following kinds of status.

Official (OF). The language (or one of the languages) of government, public services and administration, either at national, regional or local level, or all three.

Vernacular (VN). The mother tongue of some or all of the population. For most people in Britain and France, the official language is also their vernacular. But this is often not the case elsewhere, particularly in Third World countries. Hence the indications +VN or –VN in the table.

Vehicular (VL). Used for everyday non-official communication between groups speaking different vernaculars. The language in question may or may not be the mother tongue of one of these groups. It could be used, for instance, in conversations between customers and stallholders in a market in an African town that is a regional centre. If French-speaking and German-speaking Swiss communicate in English, they are using it as a vehicular language (or, to use alternative terms, a *lingua franca* or a *koine*).

Special status (SP). Sometimes (for example in North Africa) French is in wide use among the educated public, without being either an official or a vernacular language. And special status differs from vehicular status: those using French may well all have the *same* native language (e.g. Arabic). So it's not a matter of facilitating inter-group communication: the purposes for which French is used are intellectual and cultural.

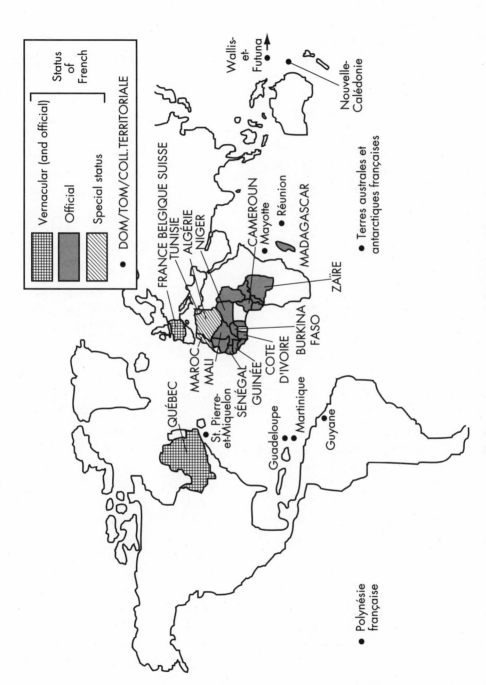

MAP 1.1 French overseas departments and territories; principal francophone states/regions (see Table 1.3)

TABLE 1.3

Country	Total population (millions)	% of francophones L1 = native speakers (and areas of concentration) L2 = second language speakers, divided when data are available into (a) a higher and (b) a lower level of competence (see p. 13)		Status of French	Other languages and status	*HDI ranking
Algeria	27.9	L2a	30	SP	Arabic OF	85th
		L2b	19		Berber VN	
Belgium	10.1	L1	41	OF	Dutch OF	
		(Wallonia, Brussels)		+VN	German OF	12th
		L2	32			
Burkina Faso	9.8	L2a	4	OF	Mandé VH	169th
		L2b	11	−VN	Dioula VH	
					local	
					vernaculars	
Cameroon	12.8	L2a	13	OF	English OF	127th
		L2b	27	−VN	local	
					vernaculars	
Canada	28.1	L1	25	OF	English OF	1st
		(Quebec, New Brunswick)		+VN	Inuit VN	
		L2	11			
France	58.3	L1	98	OF	Alsatian VN	8th
				+VN	Basque VN	
					Breton VN	
					Catalan VN	
					Corsican VN	
					Flemish VN	
					Occitan VN	
Guinea	6.7	L2a	5	OF	local	168th
		L2b	15	−VN	vernaculars	
Ivory Coast	14.2	L2a	14	OF	Dioula VH	145th
		L2b	34	−VN	Baoulé VH	
					local	
					vernaculars	

TABLE 1.3 *continued*

Madagascar	15.2	L2a	9	OF	Malagasy OF	135th
		L2b	6			
Mali	10.7	L2a	5	OF	Bambara VH	172nd
		L2b	5	–VN	Malinke VH	
					local	
					vernaculars	
Morocco	26.8	L2a	15	SP	Arabic OF	117th
		L2b	13			
Niger	9.1	L2a	3	OF	Hausa VH	174th
		L2b	8	–VN	local	
					vernaculars	
Senegal	8.3	L2a	9	OF	Wolof VH	152nd
		L2b	15	–VN	Peul VN	
Switzerland	7.3	L1	18	OF	German OF	13th
		(Fribourg, Geneva, Jura,		+VN	Italian OF	
		Neuchâtel, Valais, Vaud)			Romansch OF	
		L2	30			
Tunisia	8.9	L2a	22	SP	Arabic OF	75th
		L2b	29			
Zaire	44.5	L2a	9	OF	Chiluba VH	143rd
		L2b	30	–VN	Kikongo VH	
					Kiswahili VH	
					Lingala VH	

Sources: Philips Geographical Digest 1996–97 (col. 2), Rossillon 1995 (col. 3), UNDP Human Development Report 1995 (col. 6)

*The Human Development Index is calculated by the UN for 174 countries on a basis of the figures for national income, literacy and life expectancy. It thus gives an overall indication of levels of wealth, education and health.

Figure 1.1 (adapted from Cuq 1991 and Léger 1987) will help you to classify these various countries. The innermost circle is for the ones in which French is the vernacular of at least a substantial part of the population, as well as having official status. The second circle contains former French (or Belgian) colonies in which French is not a vernacular, but is nevertheless the official language or one of the official languages. In the third circle are former colonies where French, though no longer

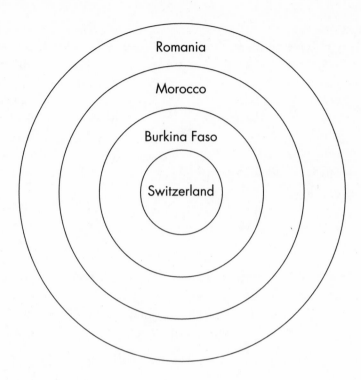

FIGURE 1.1

official, still has special status. Finally, the outer circle relates to countries in which French is much studied as a foreign language, but otherwise has no role in national life. One representative state has been inserted into each circle.

■ Insert as many other countries as you can, using their French names.

■■ Referring again to Table 1.3, why might it be more realistic to refer to 'francophone' Africa rather than to francophone Africa?

■■ Is it possible to give a definition of pays francophone which will fit all sixteen cases in Table 1.3?

■■ Consider the following countries – Burkina Faso, France, Ivory Coast, Morocco, Senegal and Switzerland – and establish as many points of similarity and difference between them as you can. Take account of the status and use of French, but also consider the importance and role of other languages, the economic, educational and health levels and the geographical location.

It should be clear by now that there are no countries in which French is a widely used vernacular without also being an official language. Conversely, there are many countries in which, although French is official, it is not widely spoken, and other languages perform the vernacular and vehicular functions. So, as an international language, French seems to owe much more to its status and prestige than it does to the extent of its use.

- Compare French with other languages from the 'top twelve' in this connection.

■■ What conclusions follow about the position of French in the world, and particularly the Third World?

■■■ Summarize the work you have been doing so far by commenting on the apparent paradox that 'the francophone world is fundamentally multilingual and multicultural'.

If 'francophone country' is a somewhat problematic concept, then it is no less difficult to decide who can properly be described as a 'francophone person'. This term can apply either to someone whose native language is French or to someone one who has learnt French as a second language. But there is no hard and fast rule specifying how competent a non-native learner has to be in order to qualify. An E grade in GCSE French probably wouldn't be regarded as making someone a 'francophone' – but what about a B at A level? Many so-called 'francophones' in Africa are much less proficient than this. In Table 1.3, the subdivision of the L2 category (second-language francophones) is intended to make the term a little less all-embracing, and is based on educational statistics for the various countries. Category (a) covers speakers who have studied French for six or more years at school; into category (b) come those who have studied it for two or more years, but may have had little occasion to use it subsequently, and whose knowledge may be quite rudimentary. Some authorities postulate a category of *francophones réels* or *véritables francophones*, corresponding to the L1 and L2a categories combined, while referring to those in the L2b category as *francophones occasionnels*.

■■ How far do such sub-categorizations go towards clarifying the situation?

Language statistics and forecasts can vary greatly according to the way in which terms like *francophone* are interpreted. Here are some contrasting predictions about the number of 'francophones' worldwide, and their projected increase (from Chaudenson 1991: 15):

> L'édition francophone ... connaît des difficultés de structures plus que de marché; le potentiel de lecteurs reste immense: presque 200 millions (*H de Kerret*).

> La francophonie est en constante expansion et en l'an 2000 il y aura 160 millions de francophones (*France-Inter*).

> On dit que 300 millions de locuteurs peuvent pratiquer le français (*Libération*).

> A ce rythme [i.e. if population growth and expansion of education continue] il y aura dans les premières décennies du XXIᵉ siècle quelque cinq cent millions de francophones (*Le Point*).

■■ What differing assumptions might account for these divergent estimates?

The more objectively based projections given in the Bordas *Atlas de la langue française* suggest an increase between 1993 and 2003 of the order of 5.5 per cent in the number of L2a speakers and 1.6 per cent in the number of L2b speakers in Africa, this being the continent where the main increase in L2 speakers is likely. The same source estimates the current world total of francophones (i.e. L1 + L2a + L2b) at 131,400,000.

■■ How justified do the above estimates and projections seem in the light of this?

Michel Guillou is one of many commentators who distinguish between the growth in absolute terms of the number of francophones and their relative stagnation as compared with other languages:

> ... la pratique de la langue française, son usage comme langue

maternelle ou langue seconde couramment utilisée, sont à la fois en progression et en déclin.

(Guillou 1993: 33)

■■ Comment on this, making as many comparisons with other languages as you can.

The francophone movement

In recent years a number of international francophone organizations and associations have grown up. Indeed, of the various francophone or partly francophone countries, only Algeria is currently a non-participant in this 'francophone movement'. Moreover, countries like Bulgaria, Egypt, Lebanon and Romania are also involved: though not generally thought of as francophone, they have their own long-standing political or cultural ties with France. Here are some basic items of documentation relating to *la francophonie*.

Main stages in its development

1880 The term *francophonie* is coined by the geographer Onésime Reclus.

1926 *Association des écrivains de langue française* founded.

1950 *Union internationale de journalistes et de la presse de langue française* founded.

1961 *Association des Universités partiellement ou entièrement de langue française* founded.

1962 Prominent figures like L. S. Senghor and Norodom Sihanouk (heads of state of Senegal and Cambodia respectively) propose a 'French-speaking union'.

1965 President Bourguiba of Tunisia calls for a 'French Commonwealth'.

1967 First meeting (in Luxembourg) of the *Assemblée internationale des parlementaires de langue française*.

1969 First conference (in Niamey, Niger) of francophone states. Outcome: the ACCT (*Association de coopération culturelle et technique*) is founded the following year.

1984 Launch of TV5, the international French-language channel. Funded by France, Belgium, Canada-Québec, and Switzerland. The *Haut Conseil de la francophonie* is set up by François Mitterrand.

1986 First 'francophone summit' (*Conférence des Chefs d'États et de Gouvernements ayant en commun l'usage du français*) meets at last in Versailles, having been discussed for twenty years. The French government creates the ministerial post of *secrétaire d'État à la francophonie*. The development of scientific and technical terminology is furthered by the founding of RINT (*Réseau international de néologie et de terminologie*), with fifteen member states.

1987 Second francophone summit held in Quebec.

1989 Third summit in Dakar (Senegal).

1991 Fourth summit in Paris: forty-seven teams of delegates attend. Cambodia, Bulgaria and Romania become members.

1993 Fifth summit in Mauritius. By now the phrase *ayant en commun l'usage du français* had been replaced by *ayant le français en partage*.

1995 Sixth summit in Cotonou (Benin).

Interest in the francophone movement has recently been rekindled in Vietnam, and it is planned to hold the seventh summit in Hanoi in 1997.

■■■ It can be seen from this outline that the francophone movement really got under way only in the 1960s. What do you think was the influence of the political developments occurring at that time (e.g. the independence of the French and Belgian colonies, Gaullist hostility towards the 'Anglo-Saxon' world)?

Popular perceptions of *la francophonie* can be somewhat vague. A recent survey (reported in *L'Année francophone internationale* 1995) revealed that 15 per cent of the French nationals interviewed were unable to name any francophone country other than France itself – 54.2 per cent managed to name Belgium, 23.4 per cent Switzerland, but only 13.9 per cent mentioned Algeria or Senegal. And funding is a perennial problem. According to *Le Monde* (2 December 1995), the overall annual budget of the francophone movement amounts to 420,000,000 F, or just 2 F per inhabitant of each member state. But the organization of the 1995 summit alone cost 200 million francs.

■■   What problems does this imply for international *francophonie*?

Ideology

Here are various declarations by leading figures which convey something of the ideology of the movement. Underlying them are an emphasis on the world-wide dissemination of the French language, and the belief that there are special links between the language and certain important cultural and political values (an idea forcefully expressed over a century ago by the historian Renan: «La liberté, les droits de l'homme, la fraternité ont pour la prèmière fois dans le monde été proclamés en français»).

> Abrégé du monde puisqu'elle comprend tous les continents, toutes les races, toutes les religions, la francophonie tend à l'universalisme (*Xavier Deniau*).

> La francophonie, c'est cet humanisme intégral qui se tisse autour de la terre, cette symbiose des énergies dormantes de tous les continents, de toutes les races qui se réveillent à leur chaleur complémentaire . . . Le français nous a séduits de ses mots abstraits et rares dans nos langues maternelles. Chacun des mots est naturellement nimbé d'un halo de sève et de sang. Les mots français rayonnent de mille feux comme des fusées qui éclairent notre nuit (*Léopold Sédar Senghor*).

> Car il est vrai que la France a de tout temps labouré avec passion le champ de l'intelligence et offert à la terre entière d'assez précieuses récoltes, il est vrai qu'elle met à la disposition du monde une langue adaptée par excellence au caractère universel de la pensée (*Charles de Gaulle*).

■■   Focusing on key words such as *universalisme, humanisme, pensée,* try to characterize the essence of the francophone ideology as it emerges from statements like these.

■■   How convincing do you find these ideas?

Some international francophone organizations and examples of practical measures (1992–93 data)

ACCT (Agence de coopération culturelle et technique)

– provision of over a million school textbooks and five libraries in Third World francophone countries
– provision of sixty training places (electronics, mechanics, computer science) for nationals of African countries
– extension of European and Canadian television coverage to Africa (TV5 Afrique)
– grants for computerization and publication of legal documents in twelve francophone countries
– organization of a major African cultural festival in Abidjan (Ivory Coast)

AIMF (Association internationale des maires et responsables des capitales et métropoles partiellement ou entièrement de langue française)

– grant (700,000F) for hospital in Brazzaville (Congo)
– similar grants for renovation of two stadia in Burkina Faso
– grant for computerizing municipal accounts in Abidjan
– gifts of reconditioned Lyons dustcarts to municipalities in Tunisia, Niger and the Comoros Islands

AIPLF (Assemblée internationale des parlementaires de langue française)

– various training courses for parliamentary archivists.

The existence of dozens of other associations should also be noted, such as: Associations des écrivains/économistes/historiens/géographes/informaticiens/sociologues de langue française.

Overall, the official analysis of 400 measures taken in 1992–93 shows the following distribution:

Education (including teacher training, buildings, exchanges, etc.)	32%
Culture (festivals, exhibitions, etc.)	23%
Economics (training schemes, industrial or agricultural projects)	17%

Health (hospital building, medical equipment, etc.)   14%
Tourism and Sport   14%

(Source: État de la francophonie dans le monde: données 1993)

■ The principal value of the francophone movement to date is its contribution to North–South co-operation. In what ways does it carry out such a role?

Perspectives and problems

North–South co-operation is not the only aim envisaged for organized *francophonie*. Consider the following remarks by the diplomat Gilbert Pérol:

> [Le français] offre, face à l'anglais dominateur, une alternative. Il est – autant mais plus symboliquement que d'autres, l'espagnol, l'allemand, l'arabe – la langue du refus du monopole anglo-américain. Parce qu'il est là... il empêche la vague de l'uniformité de tout submerger. Aussi faible que soit sa position dans certaines parties du monde... il est là, borne têtue d'un non-conformisme, d'une non-banalisation, finalement d'une non-soumission. «*Ici commence*, disaient les écriteaux dressés aux frontières de la France de Valmy, *le pays de la liberté*!» Dans les réunions internationales où s'égrène l'interminable chapelet des orateurs parlant anglais, il m'a toujours paru – bien sûr, c'est le Français qui perce en moi – que, lorsqu'un intervenant annonçait: «*Je m'exprimerai en français*», il y avait dans l'assistance un imperceptible frémissement qui était celui d'un intérêt relancé, d'une complice et fraternelle attente.

(Lettre(s), January 1993)

Valmy: battlefield in eastern France where the French revolutionary armies defeated the Prussians in 1792.

■■ Outline the advantages which the writer sees in a strong francophone presence on the world scene. As an anglophone (and perhaps also a citizen of a Commonwealth country), what do you think of his point of view?

Such thoughts were echoed on a more official level at the 1995 francophone summit, when the decision was taken to create a post of *secrétaire général de la francophonie* (with effect from 1997), the intention being to provide the member states with a spokesperson on political questions, on the model of the Commonwealth's Secretary General. The 'francophone bloc' – so far merely an economic and cultural grouping – will, it is hoped, have a more powerful voice in international politics as a result.

■■ At the time of the meeting the francophone movement was described as 'l'embêteuse du monde', and the view expressed that 'la francophonie sera subversive ou elle ne sera pas'. Can you explain what was meant?

However, there were doubts about the chances of a meaningful consensus emerging from an association whose 1995 summit was attended by:

Belgium (Kingdom of), Belgium (French Community: Wallonia-Brussels), Benin, Bulgaria, Burkina Faso, Burundi, Cambodia, Cameroon, Canada (Federal), Canada (Quebec-New Brunswick), Cap-Verde, Central African Republic, Chad, Comoros, Congo, Dominican Republic, Egypt, Equatorial Guinea, France, Gabon, Guinea, Guinea-Bissau, Haiti, Ivory Coast, Laos, Lebanon, Luxembourg, Madagascar, Mali, Mauritania, Mauritius, Moldavia, Monaco, Morocco, Niger, Ruanda, Romania, Saint-Lucia, Sao-Tomé and Principe, Senegal, Seychelles, Switzerland, Togo, Tunisia, Vanuatu, Vietnam, Zaire, and (by special invitation) a delegation from the Aosta valley in northern Italy.

■ Why did Belgium and Canada each send two delegations?

■ Why was the Aosta valley (*Val d'Aoste*) represented?

■■ Can you sort these states into sub-groupings between which there might be broader divergencies of views or differences of interest?

■■■ It is sometimes claimed that, despite the high-minded rhetoric, the francophone movement provides France with a front behind which she can maintain her hold over former colonies, and obtain more international influence than she really merits. What evidence might there be for or against this view?

■■■ Explore the parallels between the francophone movement and the Commonwealth. Keep in mind such factors as comprehensiveness of membership, the role of the British monarchy, the relative importance of linguistic, ideological, cultural, political and economic factors.

■■■ What do you think is likely to be the world status of French a century from now?

Further reading

See Asher and Simpson (1994), Bright (1992), Comrie (1987) and Crystal (1987, 1992) for general data about the world's languages, where they are spoken and by how many people. *Quid* (the annual compendium of information published by Laffont) is useful for factual information about particular countries, and so are the *Petit Robert 2* and the proper names section of the *Petit Larousse Illustré*. Ager (1995) provides a detailed survey of current linguistic, political and economic issues in the various francophone countries. See Picoche and Marchello-Nizia (1989) for a more historically oriented account. A concise overview of the franco-phone movement is also provided by Deniau (1992), and Gordon (1978) is informative about its ideological background. Muller (1985), Offord (1990) and Walter (1988) give concise outlines of the position of French around the world; there are more detailed accounts in Chaudenson (1991). An abundance of excellent maps, statistics about language use, and information on education, the media and francophone organizations is to be found in the Bordas *Atlas de la langue française* (Rossillon 1995). Guillou (1993), Léger (1987) and Rossillon (1983) are examples of more polemical approaches. Regular official updates on a variety of topics are published in *État de la francophonie dans le monde* and in *L'Année francophone internationale*.

● ● ●

Chapter 2

French as a
first language
Europe and North America

Multilingualism and language policy

Three multilingual countries are to be considered here: Switzerland, Belgium and Canada. In each of them French is the native language of a section of the population, and French-speaking communities have, for generations, lived alongside groups speaking other languages.

■   For each country, find out:

-   the official languages (and, in the case of Switzerland, the difference between an 'official' and a 'national' language)
-   the regions in which the languages are spoken
-   the number of people speaking them, and the percentage of the total population that they represent.

Multilingual nation-states need a 'language policy' that will determine the status of the languages native to their various communities, specifying which are to be used in government documents, forms and circulars, in the publicly owned media, in the educational and legal systems, in the armed forces, on road signs, in railway station announcements – perhaps even in the private business sector. The term *language planning* is applied to the process of establishing such a policy: *status planning* (the kind referred to here) is to be distinguished from *corpus planning*, which is concerned with questions of standardization and correct usage (i.e. issues like those considered in Chapters 11 and 12).

It would of course be possible to deem one language to be official throughout the country, and to relegate the others to the status of vernaculars.

■■   Such a 'monolingual' solution would have the advantage of simplicity, but what might be its disadvantages?

In each of the three countries being considered here, more than one language is given official status. There are two principles that can be followed in language planning:

Personality principle. Services are provided by the authorities in two or more official languages, and the choice of which one to use is up to the individual. This applies to central government services in each of the three countries (though the Swiss government doesn't offer federal services in Romansch). The personality principle is also in force locally in Brussels (see p. 32), in the bilingual Canadian province of New Brunswick, and in anglophone Canada wherever speakers of French account for more than 10 per cent of the population.

Territorial principle. A given territory has only one language with official status, and there is no entitlement to services in any other language. This principle applies at local (i.e. regional, cantonal or provincial) level in each of the countries, except as specified above.

■ Which would be the most appropriate principle for a hypothetical country where speakers of Language A mainly lived in, say, the western provinces, and speakers of Language B in the eastern ones?

■ What if speakers of A and B were distributed in a random way?

In real life things are less clear-cut, of course.

■■ If in each of the following places, a francophone citizen were able to use French, would it be a specific entitlement, normal language use in the place concerned, or would they simply be lucky? Why? (Use the factual information you have already obtained as a basis for your answer.)

-   a Liège police station
-   a Berne department store
-   the railway station in Zurich
-   the town hall in Ghent
-   the municipal information office in Antwerp
-   a Brussels post office
-   a hotel in Quebec City
-   the *Air Canada* office in Vancouver.

Linguistic and non-linguistic factors

Here is some non-linguistic data about the three countries. Parameters like the ones shown sometimes change significantly as time passes, so, when appropriate, data from the last century is included as well as contemporary data.

In each case, take the rudimentary notes given here as a starting point and add as much further information as you can when answering the questions.

TABLE 2.1

Belgium mid-nineteenth century	*Flanders*	devoutly Catholic; conservative; rural; underprivileged economically (known as 'la pauvre Flandre')
	Wallonia ·	nominally Catholic, but increasingly secular urban population; strong socialist movement; Hainaut and Liège provinces a cradle of the Industrial Revolution (coal, steel); one of Europe's most dynamic regions
Belgium present day	*Flanders*	still devoutly Catholic, but new industries (chemicals, electronics) and port activities make it one of the most prosperous European regions; predominantly right-wing politically
	Wallonia	still less Catholic than Flanders; old industries now declining (last coal mine closed in 1985); one of Europe's problem regions (Hainaut on a level with Ireland and Southern Italy in EU tables); predominantly left-wing politically

- Do non-linguistic divisions in Belgium reinforce the linguistic ones?

■■ Have Flanders and Wallonia become more similar since the mid-nineteenth century?

TABLE 2.2

Quebec until mid-twentieth century	Francophones	Catholic, rural, underprivileged, education run by clergy, separate legal system based on Code Napoléon
	Anglophones	Protestant, urban (mainly Montreal), in control of centres of economic power, British-type legal system
Quebec present day	Francophones	Less devout, more urbanized, and more prominent economically than in the nineteenth century, secular education introduced after World War II, but legal system still in force
	Anglophones	Still urban and nominally Protestant, but less dominant economically than previously

■   What social and cultural changes have occurred since the 1950s?

■■   The francophones of Quebec claim to be a 'distinct society' within Canada (and seek special constitutional arrangements for their province as a consequence – if not outright independence). Given these changes, do you think their claim is still justified?

TABLE 2.3

Switzerland (present day)

	French-speaking region	German-speaking region
Population (millions)	1.46 (including 1.07 francophones)	5.0 (including 4.21 germanophones)
Urbanization		
No. of cities of 100,000+ population	2	3
Proportion of land use (%)		
Woods/forests	30.3	30.9
Agriculture	40.8	43.7
Urban	9.5	10.6

continued

27

TABLE 2.3 *continued*

Highest and lowest income categories (average no. of each per canton)		
Top executives	2,169	1,703
Unskilled workers	36,091	27,599
Distribution of employment by sector (%)		
Primary	3.7	6.0
Secondary	30.1	34.9
Tertiary	62.2	56.4
Unemployed	3.3	1.7
Income		
Average per head (Swiss francs)	39,860	43,050
Education		
University graduates (average no. per canton)	67,778	41,752
Cantons by religion		
Predominantly Catholic	3	12
Predominantly Protestant	2	8

Source: Swiss Federal Statistical Office, 1994–95

Multilingual cantons: as statistics are published by cantons not by language areas, Valais has for the purposes of Table 2.3 been counted as French-speaking, Berne and Fribourg as German-speaking.

- It has often been observed that in Switzerland the language divisions between these two regions tend not to be reinforced by other social or economic divisions. What evidence for this is to be found in data of the kind given in Table 2.3?

- ■ How might this state of affairs help to explain the relative absence of inter-community conflict in Switzerland as compared with Belgium or Canada?

Case-studies: language-related rivalries

Switzerland: the Jura Crisis and the Rösti Curtain

The Helvetic Confederation is renowned for the harmony between its various communities, and we have seen that language divisions are cross-cut by religious and other cleavages. However, it is likely that the Swiss are not inherently more peaceable than any other nation, but are simply fortunate in having the particular social structures that they do. Here is an 'exception that proves the rule'.

Until 1979, Berne, the largest of the cantons, comprised two language groups: a French-speaking population in the northern third of the canton (the Jura district) and German-speakers in the southern two-thirds. There were also two religious groups: Protestants in the German-speaking area and in the south of the Jura district; Catholics in the northern Jura.

In 1947, a seemingly trivial incident concerning language use in the cantonal parliament sparked off growing discontent among francophones in the Jura (this district being a relatively declining and unprosperous watch-making region). During the 1960s and 1970s, discontent snowballed into a fully fledged separatist movement, with bombings, arson attacks and pitched battles with the police. A few demanded union with the adjacent Jura department of France in a completely autonomous 'Jura nation'; but most aimed merely at independence from the rest of Berne canton.

The issue was settled by a series of referenda at national, cantonal and local level. The outcome was that the francophone Catholics voted for independence, whereas the francophone Protestants voted (narrowly) to remain within Berne. Accordingly, a French-speaking and Catholic canton of Jura (capital: Delémont) came into being in 1979, the first new canton since 1815 (see Maps 2.1 and 2.2). Some Jurassian irredentists still lay claim to the Protestant *Jura bernois*, but by and large the crisis was defused by the various electoral consultations.

- What allegiances were revealed by the voting patterns of the inhabitants of the *Jura bernois*?

- ■ Specify how non-linguistic and linguistic factors interacted to trigger off the Jura crisis, and contrast the interrelationship of these factors in Berne with the absence of language-related conflict elsewhere in Switzerland.

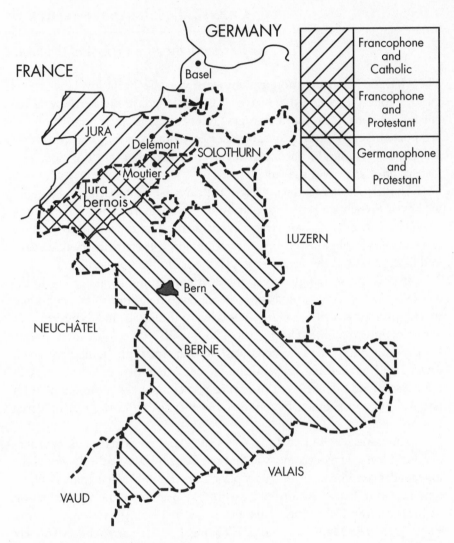

MAP 2.1   Switzerland: Jura and Berne cantons

A more recent and more generalized source of inter-community friction has in recent years been the unease felt by the 'Latin' groups and notably the French-speakers, about the increasing economic dominance of the germanophone 'Golden Triangle' district (between Zurich, Basle and Schaffhausen) and the disproportionate growth of Zurich itself. On either side of the francophone/germanophone border (the so-called *rideau de rösti* – see Map 2.2) there have been noteworthy discrepancies in

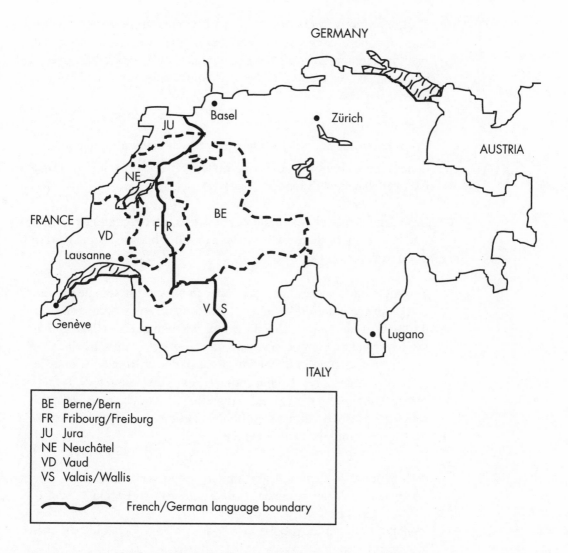

GERMANY

Basel

Zürich

AUSTRIA

JU

NE

FRANCE

VD

FR

BE

Lausanne

Genève

VS

Lugano

ITALY

BE	Berne/Bern
FR	Fribourg/Freiburg
JU	Jura
NE	Neuchâtel
VD	Vaud
VS	Valais/Wallis

French/German language boundary

MAP 2.2 Switzerland: 'the 'Rösti Curtain' and adjacent cantons

voting patterns on such issues as membership of the EU or immigration controls. And unemployment is currently lower in German-speaking Switzerland than in the Suisse Romande. So, though a little hysterical, statements like the following betray quite widespread disquiet:

> Politiquement, la Suisse romande est en train de devenir une réserve d'Indiens . . . On assiste bel et bien à une sorte de colonisation à froid.

31

> Economie, pouvoir politique, culture: la Confédération suisse bascule vers une déséquilibre croissant, par lequel les Latins se voient méthodiquement dépossédés. Cet ouvrage révèle des faits nouveaux qui prouvent la mainmise des germanophones sur l'ensemble du pays.
>
> (Grimm-Gobat and Charpilloz 1982: cover)

■ What are *rösti*, and why do they have such cultural significance?

■■ Specify how changing economic patterns are threatening to disrupt the inter-community balance.

What emerges from the following account is that inter-community friction in Switzerland is more than just a matter of rivalry between francophones and germanophones:

> Les Alémaniques ressentent de moins en moins le besoin de prendre en compte le reste de la Suisse. Les Romands ne s'occupent guère du Tessin que comme allié face aux Alémaniques, et considèrent les Romanches comme une simple curiosité ... Les Tessinois se plaignent du manque de soutien de la part des Romands, mais les imitent à l'égard des Romanches ... Les Alémaniques de la périphérie enfin pestent contre l'arrogance de Zurich, mais ils ne se soucient pas des difficultés qu'ils causent aux Confédérés en exagérant l'emploi de l'alémanique.
>
> (Giordan 1992: 204)

l'alémanique: Swiss German dialects, the use of which is increasing at the present time; *le Tessin*: the canton of Ticino (principal city: Lugano).

■ Identify the various groups referred to, their location and their languages.

■■ Try to account for their attitudes.

Belgium: The 'Brussels Oil-Stain' and the mayor who refused to speak Dutch

Along with Dutch-speaking Flanders and francophone Wallonia, the Brussels conurbation has become one of the three administrative regions of Belgium, as the country moves towards a federal system. *Bruxelles-*

VLAANDEREN

WALLONIE

Bilingual region of Bruxelles-Capitale/Brussel-Hoofdstad.
(City plus eighteen suburban boroughs: 'les dix-neuf communes').

Outer suburbs in Flanders: 'les communes périphériques'.

Boundary between Flanders and Wallonia.

Flemish boroughs providing certain French language services for francophone residents:
'les communes à facilités'.
1 Wemmel
2 Kraainem (Crainhem)
3 Wezembeek-Oppem
4 Sint-Genesius-Rode (Rhode St-Genèse)
5 Linkebeek
6 Drogenbos

MAP 2.3 Brussels and environs

33

Capitale consists of the city of Brussels itself together with eighteen suburban boroughs. This entire region (161 km², 950,000 inhabitants) has bilingual status, with all local services – from parking tickets and film subtitles to education – provided in both languages (see Map 2.3).

In practice, though, four-fifths of the Belgians resident in the capital are francophones, with particularly high concentrations – often close to 100 per cent – in the southern and eastern suburbs. Geographically, Brussels is an enclave within Flanders (the 'frontier' with Wallonia lies some 5 km to the south), and historically was itself a Dutch-speaking town, as many local place-names demonstrate. Even in the late nineteenth century, the proportion of Dutch-speaking *Bruxellois* was far higher than it is today (around two-thirds). But its role as national capital and, more recently, as a European centre, has progressively strengthened its francophone aspect, and the result has been a feeling among the Flemings that Brussels has been 'lost' to Flanders; linguistically at any rate.

Recent shifts of population – similar to those in British cities – have exacerbated this problem. As a result of immigration, there are now many inner-city districts where Arabic or Turkish are more likely to be heard than either French or Dutch. The more prosperous and predominantly francophone Belgian residents have moved further out, in many cases into villages in adjoining parts of Flanders. In some of these affluent commuter communities the francophones now outnumber the traditional Dutch-speaking residents, and are allowed bilingual facilities approximating those found in Bruxelles-Capitale itself. This francophone 'tache d'huile' is a source of disquiet in Flanders, for such extensions of the bilingual area (and the prospect perhaps of more to come) represent a further loss of monolingual territory. For the francophones, who have the support of many in Brussels and indeed in Wallonia, it is a simple matter of human rights.

In recent years these *communes à facilités* on the periphery of the conurbation proper have seen many ugly confrontations:

De temps en temps, dans ces six communes à problèmes – Drogenbos, Kraainem, Linkebeek, Rhode-Saint-Genèse, Wemmel, Wezembeek-Oppem – l'élu francophone qui s'est absenté de son domicile retrouve ses murs et son jardin couverts d'autocollants et de banderoles parfaitement clairs: *Faciliteiten weg ermee, Franskiljons pas u aan of verhuis* («Au diable les facilités», «Fransquillons adaptez-vous ou déménagez»). En mai 1993, onze cars de police, trois fourgons cellulaires et deux canons à eau furent nécessaires pour faire décamper des extrémistes flamands du TAK qui avaient investi la maison de Myriam Delacroix-Rolin, bourgmestre francophone de Rhode-Saint-Genèse. Commentaire de l'intéressée, avec, en filigrane, un début de fantasme bosniaque: «Ce n'est pas la première fois que j'ai affaire à des membres du TAK, mais j'ai été très étonnée de la violence avec laquelle ils sont arrivés et ont interpellé les membres de ma famille. Je suis inquiète face à ce climat de terreur».

(Guérivière 1994: 108)

TAK: Taal Aktie Komitee (Comité d'Action linguistique).

■■ The periphery of Brussels-Capital is a noteworthy example of a clash between the 'territorial' principle (espoused by the Flemings) and the 'personality' principle (espoused by the francophones). Explain how the two principles apply in this case.

The Fourons region (named after the half-a-dozen villages comprising it, which have names like Fouron-Le-Comte or Fouron-Saint-Martin) is a rural district in eastern Belgium with around 4,000 inhabitants, adjacent to the frontier with the Netherlands (see Map 2.4). Though originally Flemish, it became part of francophone Liège province in the early nineteenth century, and over the following century and a half developed strong francophone allegiances. In 1961, however, as a result of an adjustment of provincial boundaries, it was abruptly transferred to the Dutch-speaking province of Limburg, and French ceased to have any official status in the district.

Local discontent found a voice in fruit-grower José Happart and his Action fouronnaise pressure group, demanding reunion with Wallonia. Happart was elected mayor (*bourgmestre*) of the Fourons in 1986, but declared himself unable (or unwilling?) to speak Dutch, and was forced by central government to stand down, the territorial principle requiring mayors to conduct their business in the official language of their region. An ingenious *compromis belge* enabled him to carry on as *premier échevin faisant fonction de bourgmestre* (acting mayor, in effect).

This merely served to fan the flames, and paramilitary Flemish extremists carried out numerous protest marches, counter-demonstrations and punitive raids in the district:

29 juillet 1983: trois militaires de carrière, membres du VMO (Ordre des militants flamands), tirent des coups de feu contre la vitrine de

Chez Liliane, café francophone de Fouron-le-Comte. Bilan: six blessés dont un handicapé à vie. Apparemment, c'est José Happart, bête noire des flamingants, qui était visé. Il dit: «J'ai dormi pendant deux mois avec mon fusil chargé dans mon lit, à côté de moi. Le premier qui serait venu à la fenêtre, je ne lui aurais pas demandé son curriculum vitae, c'est un fait!»

(Guérivière 1994: 87)

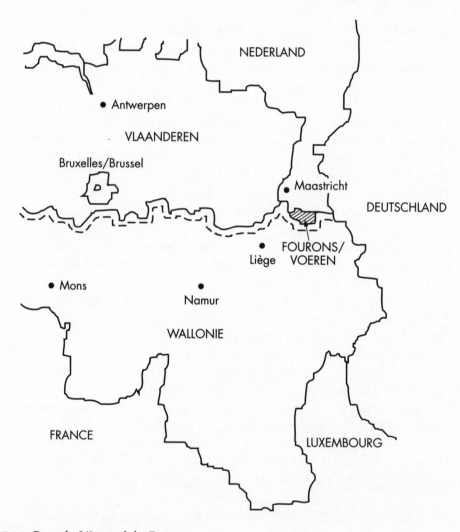

MAP 2.4 Brussels, Liège and the Fourons

In the end, various other compromises, reluctantly accepted by both sides, resulted in certain French-language facilities being granted in the Fourons, although the district still remains part of Flanders. Moreover, the economic recession of the 1990s has dampened passions down considerably. What is significant, though, is the way in which the affair dragged on for over twenty years, becoming increasingly symbolic of broader inter-community divisions, involving nationwide debate and conflict and even causing national governments to fall (Fleming and Walloon members of parliament being at odds over the issue). And Happart himself became a Euro MP and, arguably, Belgium's best-known political celebrity.

■■ Belgium was, from its foundation in 1830 until the 1980s, a highly centralized state. Switzerland has always been a confederation, with considerable autonomy for individual cantons. What bearing might this have on the fact that more heat seems to have been generated by an apparently minor crisis like the Fourons quarrel than by a relatively major one like the Jura question?

The following is from a celebrated open letter written in 1912 by the Walloon Socialist MP, Jules Destrée, to Albert I, then King of the Belgians:

> Et maintenant . . . laissez-moi Vous dire la vérité, la grande et horrifiante vérité. Vous régnez sur deux peuples. Il y a en Belgique des Wallons et des Flamands. Il n'y a pas de Belges . . . Non, Sire, il n'y a pas d'âme belge.

■■■ Explain what Destrée meant, and say whether you think his view applies to present-day Belgium. Bear in mind the national motto: L'UNION FAIT LA FORCE, and the fact that millions of Belgians from both communities turned out to pay their respects at the funeral of a later king – Baudouin I – in 1993.

Canada: La Loi 101, the Charter of the French Language

The rebirth of francophone Québécois identity during the 1960s brought the separatist Parti Québécois (PQ) to power after the 1976 provincial assembly elections. Although an autonomous Quebec state did not materialize, the PQ, shortly after the election, introduced some highly original legislation aimed at protecting and strengthening the position of the French language in the province. Going entirely against the bilingual policies of the Federal Canadian Government in Ottawa, the law (passed in 1977) states that French is the official language of Quebec. In practice, most areas of public life already operated in French, but the originality of the *Charte de la langue française*, as Bill 101 is called, lay in the attempt made to extend unilingualism to three areas in which, because of the presence of a significant anglophone minority in Quebec, English was well established: education, the private business sector, public signs.

In education, Bill 101 compelled the children of recent immigrants to attend French-language schools (previously parents had been able to choose either French- or English-language education). Private firms with more than fifty employees were required, within a specified period of time, to switch to functioning in French, and government inspectors would deliver *certificats de francisation* attesting that they had done so. Sanctions, in theory at least, included fines, public exposure and refusal of provincial government subsidies. Third, in a process sometimes referred to as *la francisation du paysage québécois*, all signs displayed in public places (including those in shops and restaurants) were required to be in French only (previously, bilingual notices had been a common enough sight, at least in Montreal with its 30 per cent anglophone population).

Not surprisingly, there were a number of appeals against the law by outraged individuals, and some of its provisions were subsequently declared unconstitutional by the Canadian Supreme Court. In particular, after much protracted wrangling, the legislation about signs was watered down to the curious compromise that, while signs outside buildings had to be in French only, 'other languages' could figure on those inside, provided a suitably prominent French text was also present.

Nevertheless, a considerable degree of success was achieved overall, so much so that there was a dramatic drop in the number of non-francophone immigrants, many anglophone businesses relocated them-selves in English-speaking Canada and there was a sizeable influx of francophones in the opposite direction. Two decades after Bill 101, the proportion of anglophones in the Quebec population had declined: currently the 7.3 million Québécois are 81.6 per cent francophone, 8.8 per cent anglophone, 8.6 per cent 'allophone' (i.e. immigrants to whom neither English nor French is native) and 1 per cent native North Americans.

Official figures (quoted in *Lettre(s)*, February 1992) reveal that in Quebec province as a whole, the percentage of native francophones rose from 80.7 per cent in 1971 to 82.9 per cent in 1986. And over the period 1971 to 1991 the proportion of anglophones claiming second-language competence in French increased from 36.7 per cent to 57.7 per cent, the equivalent increase among allophones being from 33.1 per cent to 47.4 per cent. In 1969 34.6 per cent of posts in middle and upper management were occupied by francophones and 50 per cent by anglophones; by 1988 the corresponding percentages were 58 per cent and 23 per cent. Similar trends were observed in the media. In 1960 there were eleven daily French-language newspapers with a total combined circulation of 694,300; in 1990 ten French-language papers remained, but with an increased circulation (962,600). Conversely the four English-language newspapers of 1960 (circulation 319,000) had been reduced to just two, with a circulation of 184,000.

■■ Since the 1960s, the ambitions of Quebec francophones have been summed up by the slogan: *Maîtres chez nous*. How close do you think they are, linguistically, economically and socially, to achieving their aims?

The novelist Mordecai Richler, a prominent and outspoken Montreal anglophone, describes as follows one of the effects of the Charter:

> Nineteen ninety. On a perfect summer day in Montreal . . . I went to meet some friends at a downtown bar I favored at the time: Woody's Pub, on Bishop Street. As I arrived, a solemn middle-aged man was taking photographs of the blackboard mounted on the outside steps. He was intent on a notice scrawled in chalk on the board:

TODAY'S SPECIAL

Ploughman's Lunch

> The notice happened to be a blatant violation of Quebec's Bill 178 which prohibits exterior signs in any language but French, and the photographer was one of a number of self-appointed vigilantes who, on lazy summer days off from work, do not head for the countryside to cool off in the woods or to fish; instead, they dutifully search the downtown streets for English-language or bilingual commercial signs that are an affront to Montreal's *visage linguistique* – HIYA! VERMONT BASEBALL FANS WELCOME HERE, say, or HAPPY HOUR 5 TO 7. They photograph the evidence and lodge an official complaint

with the Commission de protection de la langue française. Woody was lucky. A chalkboard sign can be erased. However, had he chosen to promote his lunches with an outside neon sign in English only, or even a bilingual one, that would have been something else again. A first offense would get him off with no worse than a warning from one of the commission's inspectors. All the same, a dossier would be opened on him. There would be another visit to his bar and, if he persisted in his obloquy, a letter from a bailiff with a thirty-day warning, and then a period of grace of up to nine months before he might be scheduled to appear in court, where he could be fined a maximum of $570.

(Richler 1992: 1–2)

■■ Speculate on the likely reactions to the sign legislation in particular and to the provisions of the Charter in general by anglophone and francophone Montréalais.

■■ Many of the appeals against the Charter were made on the grounds that the Federal constitution guarantees Canadian citizens the right to freedom of expression. Can you reconstruct the arguments?

■■■ Draw up a plan of action for an anglophone firm which, over a period of three years, is required to convert its day-to-day operation to French.

■■■ Find out more about Federal language policy and contrast it with the Quebec legislation. Relate both approaches to the two principles of language planning introduced earlier in this chapter.

The 1995 referendum for or against an independent Quebec revealed other community divisions, however. Of the anglophones, allophones and native North Americans, 95 per cent did indeed vote 'no', but less predictably, only 58 per cent of francophones voted 'yes'. A very narrow overall 'no' majority of just 53,498 votes ensured that Quebec remains part of Canada for the foreseeable future. But it has not prevented the Québécois from continuing to press for their distinctive language and culture to be formally recognized in the Federal Constitution. The Paris daily *Libération* commented:

C'est à Montréal, à plus de 50% francophone, que s'est joué le scrutin. Une analyse région par région montre ainsi une opposition entre le gros de la province, francophone, et la seule vraie métropole du Québec . . . avec environ la moitié du corps électoral . . . Ainsi . . . un comté presque entièrement anglophone comme le riche Westmount a voté à près de 80% non. Les circonscriptions à forte représentation immigrée donnent elles aussi des scores impressionnants au non. Il reste que même les comtés très francophones de Montréal n'apportent pas un soutien sans faille au camp souverainiste qui ne l'emporte que dans quatre circonscriptions. Montréal-Est la francophone a dit non à 53%. Mercier, circonscription historique du poète indépendantiste Gérald Godin, époux de la chanteuse Pauline Julien, a voté non. De même qu'Outremont, refuge des riches francophones et d'une forte communauté juive hassidim. Comme si la vision d'un Québec rural et quelque peu archaïque véhiculée par le Parti québécois butait sur la réalité multiculturelle de la ville.

(Libération, 1 November 1995)

■■ Can you account for the strong 'no' vote among allophones?

■■ What does this account suggest about the way other divisions in Quebec society cut across the language barrier, and perhaps contribute to alleviating it?

■■■ Find out as much as you can about the situation and status of French in other European states and North American regions where it has vernacular status.

■■■ Would it be fair to say that, outside metropolitan France, French is on the defensive in Europe and North America?

Further reading

Most of the titles listed at the end of Chapter 1 contain relevant material. In addition, thorough analyses of the language situations in Switzerland and Belgium are provided by McRae (1983 and 1986 respectively). For Switzerland, see also Schlaepfer (1982). Guérivière (1994) is a very readable account of language and community problems in contemporary Belgium by the Brussels correspondent of *Le Monde*. For Canada, see Sanders (1993: Chapter 13).

●　　●　　●

Chapter 3

French as a
second language
The colonial heritage

Diglossia and bilingualism

A striking feature of the francophone world is that in the majority of the countries that make it up, French is not a vernacular, but a 'second language' for its users, serving either as an official or, less commonly, as a vehicular language (see p. 8 for these terms). The following situations are characteristic of a great many Third World 'French-speaking' countries.

–   The distinction between French and other languages is not regional (as in Belgium or Canada) but functional: French is used throughout the country for specific and distinctive purposes, alternating in use with local languages. Often the 'monolingual solution' applies (cf. p. 24), with French as the sole official language.
–   Many people (the proportion varies from country to country) are not in a position to switch between a local language and French; their knowledge of the latter is limited or non-existent.

Here are some typical examples of the 'division of labour' between French and vernacular languages.

French	*Vernacular*
legal document	family conversation
TV news bulletin	folk tale
literary discourse	workmates telling jokes
obituary of national hero	angry customer in market

■   Characterize in a few words the differences between the two functions.

Not all situations are as clear-cut as these, obviously, and conventions can vary from one society to another.

■■   Group the following situations into those where a vernacular would seem appropriate, those where French would be preferable, and those where a case could be made for either:

lecture at the university	tutorial at the university
election slogan	job interview
secret meeting of terrorist group	quarrel between two motorists
the National Anthem	gossiping locals in street-
letter to a government	corner bar
department	a family reunion
televised speech by the state	conversation between school
president	friends
school maths lesson	school staff meeting.

This kind of functional differentiation between co-existing languages in the same speech community is known to sociolinguists as *diglossia*. Obviously diglossia is in no way restricted to situations involving French. English, for example, fulfils a similar role in 'anglophone' African countries.

In a diglossic situation, the non-vernacular language – the one performing the more formal role – is known as the *high* language, the other as the *low* language.

- Why, in Belgium and Switzerland, is the relationship of French to the other national languages not a diglossic one?

■■ What about the French–English and the French–Inuit relationships in Quebec?

■■ Why do the *Bruxellois* form a bilingual but not a diglossic community?

Every citizen of a diglossic society knows a vernacular or Low (L) language. Those who are lucky enough to know the High (H) as well are said to be bilingual in H and L (though in fact they are likely to have learnt their French at school, not at their mother's knee).

■■ In a diglossic society, what do you think are the disadvantages for an individual of being monolingual in L (or, conversely, the advantages of being bilingual)?

Three variations on a multilingual theme

Although diglossia is a characteristic feature of erstwhile French colonies where French remains a foreign language for the local population, there are wide differences between these countries in other aspects of language use and status. Three main categories are presented here, with examples from Africa north and south of the Sahara and from the Pacific. (The former plantation colonies in the Caribbean and the Indian Ocean, where French-based 'Creoles' have developed, are considered separately in Chapter 7.)

Variation 1

Independent countries in which French is the official language, but where numerous vernacular languages are spoken, some of which have an important vehicular role.

EXAMPLE: ZAIRE

The former Belgian Congo has been described as a 'pays linguistiquement hétérogène', and this is no understatement: some two hundred local vernacular languages and dialects are spoken in its 2,345,000 km^2 area (France is 549,000 km^2). Four of these have have the status of 'langues nationales': they are spoken over wider areas than the others and are learnt as second languages by many Zaireans (see Map 3.1). The most prominent of these vehicular languages is Lingala, spoken in and around the capital Kinshasa, where it is the undisputed 'street language'. Currently Lingala is becoming more widely used elsewhere in preference to other Zairean languages, and in oral use at any rate it has made inroads into the functions of French. Cabinet meetings are sometimes conducted in it, for instance. However, French retains the official status it had in the colonial period. (The French used in Zaire is characterized by a certain number of *belgicismes* of pronunciation and vocabulary (see p. 103). Dutch/Flemish, on the other hand, never had any significant status in the Congo).

- The languages used in Zaire might be represented diagrammatically by a triangle or pyramid, with French at the apex and the other languages at one of two different levels further down. Can you draw this?

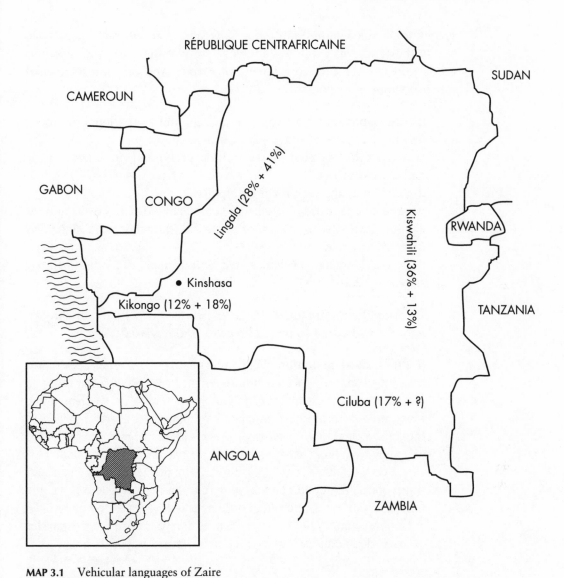

MAP 3.1 Vehicular languages of Zaire

Note: Estimated figures for L1 and L2 speakers as a percentage of the population are taken from Asher and Simpson 1994.

■■ The term *triglossia* is sometimes applied to situations where three different kinds of language status (rather than just two) are present. Can you give an account of the linguistic situation in Zaire in terms of triglossia?

French may look like the 'top' Zaire language in an abstract diagram. In reality things are probably less simple. Certainly the following functions are in principle the exclusive domain of French, and earn it a number of rather obvious 'plus points':

- it is the language of the national anthem and the national motto
- it is the language of official documents
- it is the sole language of the written press, and dominates in the audiovisual media
- it is the language used for literary writing
- it is the language used for scientific and technological writing and for communication with the rest of the world (though it increasingly has to share this role with English)
- it is the language in which the educational and administrative systems operate.

But there are 'minus points' too, as is shown in a study by M. M. Ngalasso. First, the spoken use of French is quite restricted:

> [Le français a] un nombre de locuteurs actifs relativement peu élevé, notamment par rapport aux quatre langues nationales (ce nombre de locuteurs est généralement estimé à 10 pour cent), et bénéficie d'une fonctionnalité et d'une fréquence d'emploi à l'oral très inférieures (en dehors des situations formalisées et des discours publics) à celles affectées aux langues autochtones, vernaculaires ou véhiculaires: c'est que les Zaïrois, dans leur immense majorité, quel que soit leur statut social et quelle que soit leur relation personnelle à la langue française, parlent avant tout et ordinairement (c'est-à-dire en famille, au marché, dans la rue et jusque dans la cour des écoles voire dans les bureaux de l'administration) des langues zaïroises.
>
> (Ngalasso 1994: 208–9)

Elsewhere this investigator reports that in school playgrounds in Kinshasa, even teacher–pupil conversations often take place in Lingala (Ngalasso 1988). Of conversations between government officials and members of the public, 70 per cent are in Lingala, as against 11 per cent in French. The proportions for conversations between officials themselves are 57 per cent to 31 per cent when the participants are hierarchical equals, and 67 per cent to 15 per cent between superiors and inferiors.

■■ Can you comment on the significance of these figures?

Second, the nation's official language is not afforded the respect one might have thought was due:

> En réalité, lorsque l'on regarde les choses de plus près, dans une conjoncture économique et sociale particulièrement rude pour toutes les composantes de la société zaïroise, on s'aperçoit aisément que l'association automatique de la langue française à la réussite et au pouvoir, évidente il y a seulement quelques années, apparaît aujourd'hui largement mythique. Le français langue du développement? Comment faire admettre cela quand ce qui crève les yeux de ceux qui vivent au Zaïre en ces années 90, c'est le sous-développement de plus en plus criant des villes et des campagnes, c'est la croissance des inégalités, la rupture de communication entre la classe dirigeante et la masse populaire, la montée du chômage (y compris celui, de plus en plus visible, des diplômés des universités et des grandes écoles), la chute inexorable du pouvoir d'achat des plus démunis, le sentiment généralisé que «tout est par terre», y compris la notion d'Etat, après trois décennies de campagne, en français, pour le développement national? Le français langue de la liberté et de la démocratie? Beaucoup, parmi le peuple, en sont venus à en douter, quand justement leur exclusion de l'école et leur mise au ban de la société se trouve largement attribuée à l'obstacle linguistique. Apparaît, en revanche, de plus en plus nettement, le sentiment que le français est une langue d'ostentation (faite pour exhiber un savoir strictement scolaire, cachant mal l'ignorance de la réalité des gens et de leurs problèmes), une langue d'occultation, fréquemment utilisée dans l'unique but de créer la non-transparence dans la communication, notamment entre les gouvernants et les gouvernés. Au demeurant son lien au vrai pouvoir paraît plus fictif que réel. Tous les Zaïrois le savent: pour appartenir à la sphère du pouvoir aujourd'hui, que celui-ci soit économique ou politique, il n'est pas nécessaire de parler couramment ni correctement le français: il est plus utile et plus urgent, surtout à Kinshasa, de savoir le lingala ... Les grands commerçants, comme la plupart des gens qui ont vraiment «réussi» socialement sont rarement de grands intellectuels, donc [rarement] de vrais francophones.
>
> (Ngalasso 1994: 209–10)

- Extract from this as many negative points relating to French as you can.

■■ Then compare them with the positive points enumerated earlier, and present a balanced picture of the status of French in Zaire today.

■■ Given that it is gaining ground both from French and from other local languages, how feasible would it be to make Lingala the official language of Zaire? What advantages and/or disadvantages might it have as compared with French?

Variation 2

Countries which replaced French as official language after independence, but where it still plays a major role.

EXAMPLE: THE MAGHREB (IN PARTICULAR ALGERIA)

French colonial expansion in North Africa dates from the 1830s. As a consequence of it, Algeria became administratively an integral part of France (the three departments of Alger, Constantine and Oran being added to the eighty-nine metropolitan departments). In Tunisia and Morocco, protectorates were established (in 1881 and 1912 respectively), enabling these states to preserve a degree of national autonomy. Everywhere though, French became the official language of government, administration and education. It also served an important vehicular function in such fields as business or technology, as well as being the vernacular language of around a million European settlers in Algeria, the so-called *pieds noirs*. Links with metropolitan France were further strengthened by large-scale emigration of Algerians in the opposite direction.

Various aspects of the position of French in the post-independence Maghreb countries (particularly Algeria) are evoked in the following six excerpts from the weekly Paris news magazine *L'Express* (Hoche 1994: 92–3):

– A policy of 'arabization' was introduced in all three countries. Arabic replaced French as the official language, with some noteworthy effects:

La première promotion de bacheliers entièrement «arabisés» est sortie des lycées algériens en juin 1989. S'il est évident que les jeunes de moins de 25 ans, c'est-à-dire la majorité de la population, s'expriment aujourd'hui d'abord en arabe, il n'en reste pas moins que le français demeure solidement implanté chez les plus de 40 ans ... Pour la majorité de ceux qui avaient accompli leur scolarité au moment de l'Indépendance, l'usage du français ne relève pas d'un choix. Dès le primaire, cette langue leur a été inculquée au détriment de l'arabe.

promotion: year group, in school or university.

■ What is meant by the phrase *bacheliers entièrement 'arabisés'*?

■■ Why is there a linguistic difference between those under and those over 40, and what is its significance as regards the prospects of French in Algeria?

– Some details of the legislation are as follows:

... l'Assemblée nationale algérienne, émanation exclusive du FLN, s'est prononcée ... sur la «généralisation de la langue arabe». Cette loi stipule notamment la rédaction en arabe de tous les actes et documents officiels, l'arabisation totale de l'enseignement avant 1997, celle des enseignes – sauf dans les centres touristiques classés – et de la publicité, ainsi que la traduction ou le sous-titrage en arabe des films et téléfilms et des émissions culturelles et scientifiques diffusées par la télévision. Les délibérations et débats officiels, ainsi que les réunions politiques, doivent être également en arabe, ainsi que les journaux populaires, exception faite de ceux destinés à un public étranger et des publications à caractère scientifique ... La loi prévoit que ceux qui ne la respecteront pas seront poursuivis et risqueront des peines d'amende de 1 000 à 5 000 dinars (500 à 1 000 francs environ), voire une peine de prison pouvant atteindre cinq ans.

■ Can you now give a definition of arabisation?

■■ Why do you think language legislation was still in the process of being introduced a quarter of a century after Independence?

– Arabization is closely linked with the ideological and political struggle currently taking place in Algeria:

Champion de l'«authenticité arabo-musulmane», le mouvement intégriste se bat ... depuis des années, contre l'usage du français et ses références culturelles. Les «barbus» – qui ont déjà obtenu la suppression de la mixité dans les facultés et à l'école secondaire – veulent imposer l'arabisation dans tout l'enseignement ... Sous la pression des intégristes ... les députés algériens, qui utilisent souvent le français, parlent parfois mal l'arabe et envoient leurs enfants dans les lycées français, ont donc voté à une écrasante majorité une loi qu'ils auront sans doute eux-mêmes bien du mal à respecter.

■ Why are the Islamic fundamentalists in favour of complete arabization?

■■ Why is the Algerian government in a paradoxical position as regards the status of French (heirs of the Independence movement of the 1950s and 1960s, but opponents of fundamentalism)?

– To speak of replacing French by Arabic is to oversimplify, since the vernacular varieties spoken in the Maghreb are very different from standardized literary Arabic, which is the official language elsewhere in the Arab world.

Interdire le français? «Ce serait une grave erreur ..., affirme un journaliste du quotidien *El Moudjahid*, qui n'est d'ailleurs plus le seul journal en langue française. La majorité du peuple algérien ne comprend pas l'arabe littéraire employé par les présentateurs de la télévision et préfère lire un journal écrit en français ou regarder une chaîne de télévision française. Comment arabiser l'Algérie, alors que la plupart des foyers sont équipés d'une antenne parabolique et consomment à longueur de soirée des émissions venues de France?»

■■ What would you imagine to be the respective advantages and disadvantages, as official languages, of the two types of Arabic?

– Moreover, it is by no means the case that even *arabe dialectal* is the native language of all Algerians:

Les Berbères, attachés à leur région et à leur culture ... ont marqué leur détermination à parler et à écrire leur langue, le tamazight,

pratiqué par 25% de la population algérienne ... Ils sont peu dis-
posés à céder, et représentent une force alternative qui élargit le
champ politique et complique le jeu des intégristes.

- Tamazight, though perhaps the best known, is just one of a number
  of Berber languages (Kabyle is another). These are quite distinct from
  Arabic. Where are they spoken?

■■ Why does the existence of the Berber languages indirectly serve the
  cause of French?

– For many in the Maghreb, French represents an essential link with
  the modern, secular world.

Une enquête récente menée à l'université Bab Ezzouar, à la
périphérie d'Alger, démontre bien, chez les étudiants de première
année, les paradoxes de l'arabisation. Sur plus de 800 étudiants
sondés, tous arabisés, moins de 10% souhaitent suivre leur cursus
universitaire en langue arabe. La grande majorité avoue préférer
le français, parce que le matériel d'enseignement est plus facilement
disponible dans cette langue, mais aussi pour des raisons de
débouchés sur un marché du travail saturé.

- What 'paradoxical' aspects of arabization are referred to here?

The extent to which French and Arabic seem to open up different 'thought
worlds' was shown in the following psycholinguistic test carried out in
Morocco (no doubt similar responses would have been obtained in Algeria
or Tunisia).

The respondents were eighty ... bilinguals (thirty-eight females and
forty-two males) of ages ranging from fifteen to forty, and originating
from various parts of Morocco; they included schoolchildren,
students, teachers, secretaries and professional people. They were
given a list of thirty incomplete sentences in one language and asked
to complete them in any way they wished [e.g. 'The future depends
on ... ']. Then, six weeks later, they were given the corresponding
incomplete sentences in the other language, and again asked to
complete them. Some respondents were given the French versions
of the sentences on the first occasion, and some the Arabic ones. The

six-week interval was used in order that the respondents, when completing the second set of sentences, would not immediately recall what they had written in their earlier completions. [There follow] some of the . . . contrasts between the French and the Arabic versions in each case.

FRENCH: One needs a good job to live happily.
ARABIC: One needs a good job to be able to spend one's last days praying in the mosque.

FRENCH: Rich people can afford whatever they like.
ARABIC: Rich people can afford to help their Muslim brothers.

FRENCH: The future depends on education.
ARABIC: The future depends on luck and chance.

FRENCH: A woman without children is unhappy.
ARABIC: A woman without children accepts her fate and worships God all the time.

FRENCH: My aim in life is to be a brilliant figure in society.
ARABIC: My aim in life is to leave my parents contented with me.

FRENCH: One needs a good job to live better.
ARABIC: One needs a good job to work for one's country.

FRENCH: When we have guests, we give them a drink.
ARABIC: When we have guests, we feed them very well.

. . . It seems then that the same bilingual may be able to adopt two rather different views of the world; in fact, he may experience something like what Julien Green, the French–English bilingual writer, felt on switching languages: 'it was as if, writing in English, I had become another person'.

(Bentahila 1983: 40–8)

■■ What cultural values and attitudes do French and Arabic respectively appear to represent for these bilingual speakers?

■■■ Referring both to the colonial and to the post-colonial periods, apply the concepts of *diglossia* and *bilingualism* to the language situation in the Maghreb.

■■■ In what ways does the rivalry between the French and Arabic languages in Algeria reflect the current conflict between a Westernized, francophone group and a traditionalist Islamic movement?

Variation 3

Overseas territories where French, the official language of the Republic of which they are part, co-exists with various low-status vernaculars.

EXAMPLE: NEW CALEDONIA

The sub-tropical island of New Caledonia, together with a number of small dependent islands, forms an archipelago of 37,000 km² situated in the Pacific about 2,200 km northeast of Sydney (see Map 3.2). It became a French colony in 1853 and today has the status of a *territoire d'outre-mer* (TOM), the difference between a 'colony' and a 'territory' being perhaps more one of nomenclature than of substance. Like a *département d'outre-mer* (DOM), a TOM sends elected representatives to the National Assembly and Senate in Paris, and is fully assimilated to metropolitan France as far as foreign policy and defence are concerned. Unlike the DOM, which are run on the same basis as the metropolitan departments, with a Paris-appointed prefect, New Caledonia has an *congrès territorial* with a locally elected president, and enjoys considerably more autonomy in internal matters.

Many colonial features have remained intact linguistically and socially, as well as administratively. The indigenous Melanesian islanders (*les Kanaks*), who have preserved much of their traditional family and clan organization, form 45 per cent of the overall population of 133,000, and as many as twenty-eight different Melanesian vernacular languages are used in the archipelago (none of them with more than a few thousand speakers). The non-Melanesian population, all of whom arrived after colonization, consists basically of settlers of European origin (*les Caldoches*) – either *colons libres* or descendants of inmates of the penitentiary which was such a dominant feature of nineteenth-century New Caledonia. But many individuals of mixed ethnic origin have become assimilated to the Caldoche group, and in recent years so have others with Japanese, Indonesian, Vietnamese or Polynesian (e.g. Tahitian or Vanuatuan) ancestry. The arrival of many of the latter groups coincided with the sudden expansion of nickel mining on the island in the late 1960s, a development which encouraged a further wave of settlers from metropolitan France (the so-called

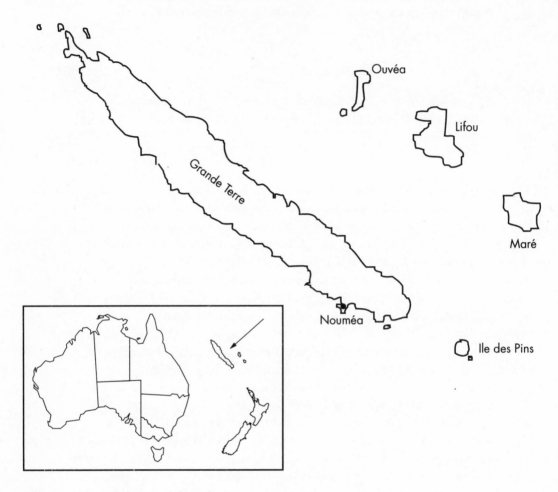

MAP 3.2 New Caledonia and dependencies

Métropolitains). So who actually counts as a Caldoche is something of a moot point these days: however, the non-Melanesian population has long been predominantly francophone, and is becoming overwhelmingly so, as younger speakers turn away from the Asian or Polynesian languages used by their parents. Nouméa (56,000 inhabitants), the capital, with a Melanesian population of only 21 per cent, is the Caldoche stronghold (as its nickname, 'Nouméa-la-Blanche', implies). Some of the minor islands, by contrast, are close to 100 per cent Melanesian.

French is, of course, the official language of New Caledonia, as it is of every DOM and TOM. It dominates the education system (despite a few concessions to the local languages), the legal system, the administration and the media, though it often takes on a strongly regional, non-standard form. French is the vernacular language of half the population, and a vehicular language for almost all of the rest (in the 1989 census, 93.7 per cent of Caledonians claimed competence in speaking, writing and reading French).

The crucial role played by French has been investigated by Mireille Darot and Christine Pauleau:

> *Discours coutumier en français soutenu.* Les visites dans les tribus sont généralement retransmises au journal télévisé, et l'on peut voir, collier de fleurs autour du cou, ... les reponsables politiques francophones natifs ... et les personnalités métropolitaines venues assurer de leur soutien leurs amis du Territoire respectant dans leurs interventions, en français soutenu, les règles non verbales du discours coutumier (la distance entre les interlocuteurs principaux croît en fonction de l'importance de la position hiérarchique, l'abaissement du regard marque le respect) ainsi que les règles verbales (courbe intonative basse et plate pour signifier le respect, utilisation de paraboles pour l'exposition d'un thème). La réponse du chef de tribu ne se distingue alors que par son degré de compétence (phonétique et syntaxique) de la langue française. Ce n'est que lorsqu'il l'ignore totalement qu'un membre de la tribu traduit en français son discours prononcé en vernaculaire.
>
> (Darot and Pauleau 1993: 287)

coutumier: in accordance with traditional tribal custom.

■   Say what kind of ceremony is being described here, and summarize the pattern of language use.

■■   What is striking about the pattern?

> *Santé.* Les familles accompagnant les malades et leur rendant visite, les aidant éventuellement à traduire leurs maux, les hôpitaux sont des lieux plurilingues par excellence dans lesquels le français de par les différentes fonctions qu'il y exerce connaît des réalisations extrêmement diversifiées d'un point de vue linguistique. Celles-ci s'inscrivent dans un *continuum* qui va du français standard de la

langue administrative à des variétés «stabilisées»: français régionaux de Métropole et français calédoniens pour une partie du personnel et des malades, et des variétés «instables» où la maîtrise et l'approximation varient en fonction de l'âge et du sexe: français langue seconde pour les malades de la brousse, des Iles, de Wallis, jusqu'à un pidgin hospitalier que les infirmières déclarent utiliser pour se faire comprendre des malades faiblement francophones.

(Darot and Pauleau 1993: 289)

■ What kind of language would you expect to be spoken by the following categories of patient, and why?

the manager of the Nouméa Crédit Lyonnais

a Kanak bus-driver

a cleaning lady from Nouméa

a small farmer from one of the offshore islands

a ferry captain

a waiter in a café in a coastal resort

an unemployed labourer

a tribal chief.

■■ Can you explain the distinction made here between *français stabilisé* and *français instable*?

Français, langue de la politique. Le français est la langue véhiculaire de l'action politique, quel que soit son objectif, indépendance ou maintien de la Calédonie dans la République. Le programme du Front de Libération Nationale Kanak et Socialiste (FLNKS) exhorte, en français, à lutter contre le colonialisme français. Il reconnaît au français la fonction de langue des relations internationales de la future Kanaky avec ses voisins anglophones. Les mots d'ordre sont élaborés en français puis traduits dans les langues vernaculaires. Lorsqu'une tribu accueille une réunion du FLNKS, le discours coutumier est confié à un militant de la tribu qui connaît le vernaculaire de la tribu, le chef répond en vernaculaire. Les échanges qui suivent se déroulent en français. Langue seconde pour la plupart des intervenants, celui-ci connaît des variations, imputables en partie à la langue première des intervenants.

(Darot and Pauleau 1993: 293)

This passage refers to the 'troubles' on New Caledonia in the late 1980s. An independence movement supported by large sections of the Melanesian population was paralleled by the emergence of a loyalist movement among the Caldoches; there was violence and conflict between the groups and with the authorities. Discussions are still continuing about the status of the island and a possible transition towards independence.

■■ For what reasons do you think the Kanak separatists choose to conduct their business in French? What is ironic about their choice?

■ Taking the last three excerpts together, list the various factors that make French the unchallenged official and vehicular language in New Caledonia.

■■ How typical an example is New Caledonia of a diglossic society?

■■■ The three variants of multilingualism that have just been illustrated are obviously not hard and fast categories. However, to a greater or lesser extent, other Third World 'francophone' countries approximate to one or another of them. Consider some, saying which category fits them best, and how closely.

■■■ Colonial languages seem to be tenacious institutions, even years after decolonization. Why should this be so, and what factors would need to be present for a colonial language to be replaced by a vernacular?

■■■ French is seen by many in the Third World as being *une langue de domination*. What is meant by this expression and how justified is it?

Further reading

See the recommended reading for Chapter 1. Other useful material is to be found in the collections of articles edited by de Robillard and

Beniamino (1993) and Abou and Haddad (1994). For a general presentation of diglossia and bilingualism, see Fasold (1984), Holmes (1992) or Wardhaugh (1992).

•   •   •

Exploring linguistic variation

Chapter 4

Languages,
dialects and *patois*

A multilingual territory

The official language of Roman France (and eventually its most widely used vernacular) was Latin. After the collapse of the Empire in the fifth century AD, Latin evolved in different ways in different regions of 'Gaul', and before long these varieties became mutually incomprehensible, having evolved into:

–   A group of southern dialects, with *oc* as their equivalent of 'yes': hence the collective name *langue d'oc*.
–   A northern group of *langue d'oïl* dialects: in the Middle Ages these had *oïl* (an early form of *oui*) for 'yes'.
–   An intermediate *franco-provençal* group.

Here are illustrations of the first two groups (not necessarily in the above order). The *oc* examples are from (a) Provence and (b) Gascony (SE and SW France respectively), the *oïl* examples from (a) Champagne (NE France) and (b) Wallonia (S Belgium).

1   (a)   C'ée mouè qu'éj li ai dounné ène chanson pour ieux chanter.
    (b)   Foyou après foyou, di djanvîr à décimbe, c'èst zèls, chaque a toûr, qu'ont adjèrcî, lès abitouwéls pitits mèssèdjes.

2   (a)   A la pastorala se mesclavan pasmens d'aigri dissonàncias, lo bruch de la guèrra s'ensaurava darrier li montanhas et detràs li flumes.
    (b)   Tot d'un còp, que sentic soma ua trucada dens lo cap e ua umbra, adarron, que traversèc sa jòia.

■   Which pair is northern (*oïl*) and which southern (*oc*)? How you can tell?

■   Which group do you think present-day 'standard' French belongs to?

■   Referring to the *Petit Larousse* if necessary, distinguish between the administrative region (and former province) known as Languedoc and the *langue d'oc* language area.

Here are two examples of *franco-provençal*:

(a) Kane i soflè l'vene, fâ sè garda li foua (Grenoble region of France)
(b) Vo n'âi rein qu'à alla de clli côté, tant qu'à vo sèyî derrâi la méson à mon oncllio (Lausanne region of Switzerland)

■ Can you spot any of the features that make these dialects 'inter-mediate' between *oïl* and *oc*?

■ Why is the Franco-Swiss frontier (and the Franco-Belgian one in the earlier examples) irrelevant to the dialect groupings?

In a survey of language use conducted at the time of the French Revolution, around twenty such local speech-forms were listed:

> ... le <u>normand</u>, le <u>picard</u>, le wallon, le champenois, le <u>messin</u>, le franc-comtois, le <u>bourguignon</u>, le <u>bressan</u>, le <u>lyonnais</u>, le <u>dauphinois</u>, l'<u>auvergnat</u>, le <u>poitevin</u>, le <u>limousin</u>, le provençal, le languedocien, le <u>velayan</u>, le <u>béarnais</u>, le <u>rouergat</u>, le gascon.

■ The underlined dialects have not been mentioned here so far. Where would each have been spoken? (The *Petit Larousse* and/or *Petit Robert* will help you to track them down.)

■ Which, on geographical grounds, would you say were *oïl* varieties, which *oc*, and which *franco-provençal*?

A number of other languages have also long been spoken in what is now metropolitan France (see Sanders 1993 for concise accounts).

■ Match each of the 'regional languages' listed below under (1) with:

- the *département(s)* where it is spoken (choose from list 2)
- a brief characterization (from 3)
- an illustrative sentence (from 4).

1   *alsacien, basque, breton, catalan, corse, flamand, francique.*
2   Bas-Rhin, Corse-du-Sud, Côtes-d'Armor, Finistère, Haut-Rhin,

Haute-Corse, Morbihan, Moselle, Nord, Pyrénées-Atlantiques, Pyrénées-Orientales.

3 (a) a Celtic idiom, closely related to the now extinct Cornish and also to Welsh; brought to France by Celts from Britain fleeing Anglo-Saxon incursions

   (b) a group of Germanic dialects, related to those spoken in south-west Germany

   (c) another Germanic idiom, this time closely related to Dutch and Low German

   (d) a language with no known affinities, though a link with languages of the Caucasus (Georgian, etc.) has been suggested

   (e) a Latin-derived language, intermediate between *langue d'oc* and Castilian Spanish

   (f) another Latin-derived group of dialects, this time having close links with Italian

   (g) yet another Germanic speech-form, known in English as *Frankish*, closely related to one of the official languages of Luxembourg

4 (a) *Se vo un sapete ciò che vo avete a fà à manghjà oghje, v'aghju à dà un' idea.*

   (b) *Mei Sprooch dat is ouser Land, der Boddem unner ousen Féiss.*

   (c) *Gouzout a rane vefe start ar c'hrogad adal ma klaskfe a dud difenn o labour e korn-bro Lanuon.*

   (d) *T'is misschien vertlooren vlaemsch, maer de Waelsch hebben't zoo noodig.*

   (e) *Oc, lo conselh, commençan per parlar lo francés; e al cap d'una mieja ora, a-n-aquel moment parlam lo patoès.*

   (f) *Mendixketan erbiak eta oreinak bakanak gelditzen dira. Beherago untxiak, galeperak eta ahateak.*

   (g) *És un foradet molt petitó, però si no el tapeu de seguida, anirà eixamplant-se i llavors hi passarà la pluja.*

   (h) *Geh nunter un schiess s'Auto uff, nemmsch min Valisel rüss un bringsch mer's uff. Ich hab Eych alle abbs mitgebrocht.*

The various *langue d'oc* dialects also have the status of a 'regional language', and are nowadays collectively referred to as *occitan*. An example sentence is included in (4).

■■ Add information about Occitan to (2) and (3) above.

■■ Summarize the work you have done by specifying the differences between:

français, francique, langue d'oïl, occitan, langue régionale.

From one kind of monolingualism to another

Since the Middle Ages, increasing political centralization and the growing cultural and economic importance of the Paris region means that the speech of the Ile-de-France – previously just one variety among many – has gradually come to be used throughout the Hexagon, and to dominate the other varieties. Language use, in other words, has *shifted* in favour of French. But all the *oïl* and *oc* dialects listed above, as well as the various regional languages, were *maintained* in use until at least as recently as the mid-nineteenth century:

> In 1863, according to official figures, 8,381 of France's 37,510 communes spoke no French; about a quarter of the country's population. The Ministry of Public Instruction found that 448,328 of the 4,018,427 schoolchildren (ages seven to thirteen) spoke no French at all, and that another 1,490,269 spoke or understood it but could not write it, suggesting an indifferent grasp of the tongue. In 24 of the country's 89 departments, more than half the communes did not speak French, and in six others a significant proportion of the communes were in the same position. In short, French was a foreign language for a substantial number of Frenchmen, including almost half the children who would reach adulthood in the last quarter of the century.
>
> (Weber 1979: 67)

■ Where do you suppose these non-francophone communes would have been located?

Here, by way of contrast, are some statistics for the mid- to late twentieth century. Only very approximate figures are given, because reliable data for the second column are difficult to obtain (how competent does one have to be to count as a 'speaker'?). Moreover, language areas (column 3)

TABLE 4.1

Language	Number of speakers	Population of region
Alsatian	1,000,000	1,620,000
Auvergnat	500,000	1,300,000
Basque	90,000	230,000
Breton	600,000	1,500,000
Catalan	200,000	360,000
Corsican	150,000	250,000
Flemish	100,000	350,000
Franco-provençal	30,000	1,240,000 (France)
Frankish	200,000	400,000
Norman	700,000	3,000,000
Occitan	1,500,000	13,000,000
Picard	2,000,000	5,500,000

Sources: Kloss and McConnell 1984, Kloss, McConnell and Verdoodt 1989, Commission of the European Communities 1986

do not always have clearly defined boundaries. (N.B. In no case is the proportion of monolingual speakers greater than 5 per cent).

■   Tentative though some of these figures may be, they point to striking developments since the 1860s as regards language maintenance and language shift. Can you give a summary?

■■   Give a brief account of the current situation along the lines of Weber's (1979) characterization of the nineteenth-century one.

Two excerpts follow which reflect this transformation of language use during the last century and a half. The first is from the most popular children's book of late nineteenth-century France, *Le Tour de France par deux enfants*. In search of a long-lost uncle, two young brothers travel round the Republic (newly re-established after the Franco-Prussian War of 1870–71). At one point they stay overnight in a village inn south of Lyons:

L'hôtelière était une bonne vieille, qui paraissait si avenante, qu'André, pour faire plaisir à Julien, se hasarda à l'interroger, mais elle ne comprenait que quelques phrases françaises, car elle parlait à l'ordinaire, comme beaucoup de vieilles gens du lieu, le patois du midi.

André et Julien, qui s'étaient levés poliment, se rassirent tout désappointés.

Les gens qui entraient parlaient tous patois entre eux; les deux enfants, assis à l'écart et ne comprenant pas un mot à ce qui se disait, se sentaient bien isolés dans cette ferme étrangère. Le petit Julien . . . dit tout bas: «Pourquoi donc tous les gens de ce pays-ci ne parlent-ils pas français?»

– C'est que tous n'ont pas pu aller à l'école. Mais dans un petit nombre d'années il n'en sera plus ainsi, et par toute la France on saura parler la langue de la patrie.

En ce moment, la porte d'en face s'ouvrit de nouveau; c'étaient les enfants de l'hôtelière qui revenaient de l'école.

– André, s'écria Julien, ces enfants doivent savoir le français, puisqu'ils vont à l'école. Quel bonheur! nous pourrons causer ensemble.

(Bruno 1877: 161–2)

Second, from Pierre-Jakez Hélias' account of his 1920s childhood in a village in western Brittany:

Le recteur et le vicaire nous parlent toujours en breton bien qu'ils soient capables de discourir en français, dit-on, aussi bien que les avocats de Quimper. Les instituteurs ne parlent que français bien que la plupart d'entre eux aient parlé le breton quand ils avaient notre âge et le parlent encore quand ils rentrent chez eux. D'après mes parents, ils ont des ordres pour faire comme ils font. Des ordres de qui? Des «gars du gouvernement». Qui sont ceux-là? Ceux qui sont à la tête de la République. Mais alors, c'est la République qui ne veut pas du breton? Elle n'en veut pas pour notre bien. Mais vous, mes parents, vous ne parlez jamais français. Personne dans le bourg ni à la campagne ne parle français, à part cette malheureuse madame Poirier. Nous n'avons pas besoin de le faire, disent les parents, mais vous, vous en aurez besoin. Il y a encore des vieux qui ne savent ni lire ni écrire. Ils n'avaient pas besoin de le savoir. Nous, nous avons eu besoin. Et besoin aussi de parler français à l'occasion. Seulement à l'occasion. Vous, vous en aurez besoin tout le temps. Qu'est-ce qui s'est passé, alors? C'est le monde qui change d'une génération à l'autre. Et qu'est-ce que je vais faire de mon breton? Ce que vous en faites maintenant avec ceux qui le savent, mais il y en aura de moins en moins.

(Hélias 1975: 206)

■■ Using these descriptions, characterize the stages of language shift in provincial France – from monolingualism in a regional language or dialect to monolingualism in French.

In 1880–81 (under the Third Republic) legislation was introduced which provided free and compulsory primary education throughout France. French was of course the sole language used in the new State school system.

■ What echoes of this are to be found in the above excerpts?

■■ Why was this development so effective in spreading standard French?

Terminology: *langue, dialecte, patois*

These three terms sometimes overlap, but basically they convey different perspectives and implications. Here are four illustrations of their use.

(a) La <u>langue</u> occitane a quatre <u>dialectes</u> principaux: le provençal, le languedocien (souvent considéré comme la forme standard), le limousin et le gascon.

La <u>langue</u> bretonne en a quatre aussi, les <u>dialectes</u> parlés dans les régions de Cornouailles, Vannes, Tréguier et Léon.

Au Moyen Age, le normand, le picard, le champenois et certains autres <u>dialectes</u> de la <u>langue</u> d'oïl avaient autant de prestige que le *francien* parlé en Ile-de-France (l'ancêtre du français moderne, et lui aussi un dialecte d'oïl).

■ What distinction between *langue* and *dialecte* emerges from these statements?

(b) When members of the same group of dialects come to differ in prestige and/or degree of standardization, however, there is often a shift in the implication of the term *langue*. Given the situation described in the last quotation, it would be inappropriate to refer to medieval Norman, Picard or Champenois as '*francien* dialects' or 'dialects of the *francien* language'. Today, though, their descendants might well be described as 'French dialects' or 'dialects of the French language'. (Conversely it would be extremely odd to claim that 'French is a dialect of Picard'.) The implication is that French has become a language, but that Norman, Picard and the rest haven't.

■ Why should this be so?

■ What differences in implication can you detect between these two statements (from tourist guidebooks)?

–   In Provence, a local dialect, Provençal, is still in circulation.
–   The Provençal language can still be heard in the countryside of Provence.

■■ Can you explain the old joke that 'a language is a dialect with an army and a navy'?

(c) Dialects of the same language obviously must be closely related to one another. This invalidates some of the following statements, even though they are quite often made:

–   Basque is a dialect of French
–   Breton is a dialect of French
–   Catalan is a dialect of French
–   Champenois is a dialect of French
–   Flemish is a dialect of French
–   Gascon is a dialect of French
–   Walloon is a dialect of French.

■ Which of these are inaccurate and why?

■ Which might be defended, and on what grounds?

(d)   All seven of the 'speech-forms' mentioned in (c) are sometimes referred to indiscriminately as *patois*, even by their own speakers as in this interview with a dialect speaker from the Vosges:

> – Pour vous, le patois, c'est une langue?
> – Non, c'est pas une langue. C'est du patois. Le dialecte, c'est un dialecte; le patois, c'est un patois; pis une langue, c'est une langue.
> – Quelle différence vous faites entre . . .
> – Je fais une différence, c'est que la langue elle a une grammaire, elle a des règles, le patois n'en a pas.
> – Y a pas de règles?
> – Non. On le dira n'importe comment, personne n'est *répréhensible*. Tandis que du français, faut le causer correctement, l'allemand, faut le causer correctement: ça c'est des langues. Tandis que le patois et le dialecte, c'est pas des langues.
> – Le patois n'a pas de règles. Comment vous conjuguez les verbes?
> – Bah! On n'a pas de verbes! On n'a pas de verbes! On cause comme ça, on *tape dans le tas*. On cause comme ça, comme on sait, mais y'a pas de règles.

(Mougin 1991: 91)

répréhensible: evidently a slip of the tongue for *responsable*.

- ■ What seem to be the implications of the term *patois*?

- ■ For such a speaker, what are the defining characteristics of a *langue* (as opposed to a *patois* or *dialecte*)?

- ■■ Why do defenders of Alsatian, Basque, Breton, Catalan, Corsican, Flemish and Occitan take strong exception to the label *patois* when it is applied to these languages?

- ■■ Summarize the meanings and implications of *langue*, *dialecte* and *patois*.

Dialects and regional languages: some recent investigations

Oïl dialects still have quite wide currency in regions like the Nord-Pas-de-Calais or neighbouring Wallonia, but received wisdom has it that in large areas of Normandy, Champagne, Touraine and Anjou, as well as in the Lyons–Grenoble area and the Suisse Romande, dialects have all but lost their identity today. At best, certain of their features survive in local *français régionaux* spoken by monolingual francophones (see Chapter 5).

However, it may be that dialects, even in these areas, have been maintained to some extent. It is a curious fact that, a hundred years ago, they were reported to be spoken largely 'by old people' – and are still so reported today. Perhaps younger people acquire a covert knowledge of them. Something of the sort seems to emerge from an investigation conducted in the late 1980s into the survival of dialect in the Calvados *département* of Lower Normandy:

> – ch'est pas ch' que no crait (= ce n'est pas ce qu'on croit): j'ai entendu un jeune garçon de 8 ans réaliser cette séquence, à ma grande surprise parce qu'il s'exprimait quotidiennement en français, à ma connaissance du moins et je le connaissais bien. Nous étions dans une cour de ferme . . . devant un élevateur électrique qui venait de tomber en panne. Je crois avoir compris que ce jeune fils de culti-vateur s'amusait à parodier – en dialecte – un discours archaïque vilipendant la modernisation des techniques agricoles (le discours de son grand-père, peut-être, qui parle volontiers ainsi) . . .
>
> – les cônelles sont pas bié tiérues, pa là (les corbeaux ne sont pas très forts, par ici): . . . j'emmenais il y a deux ans en Irlande un neveu de 16 ans et un de ses camarades du même âge, tous deux fils de cultivateurs; tous deux s'expriment quotidiennement en français, même s'ils ont une connaissance virtuelle mais parfaite du patois. Le dépaysement linguistique, mêlé à la bonne humeur des vacances leur a fait réaliser durant ce séjour une foule d'énoncés de ce type, le plus souvent accompagnés de fous rires, et presque toujours de jurons locaux jubilatoires. Je ne leur supposais pas une telle compétence.
>
> (Boissel 1991: 23–4)

The investigator concludes:

> Dira-t-on . . . qu'il s'agit du stade ultime d'une pratique dialectale, alors que ces moments très fréquents en conversation représentent le coeur du langage, le théâtre dans la langue, le plaisir de parler?
>
> (Boissel 1991: 25)

- ■ Characterize the kind of language maintenance being described here.

■■ Is the writer justified in his optimism about the survival prospects of this Norman dialect?

The view that one can never be quite sure that a dialect really is threatened by extinction is forcefully expressed in the following:

> ... En Bretagne romane, je l'ai vérifié moi-même, le patois local d'oïl reste usuel dans les familles rurales, même pour une partie des enfants, et même si des locuteurs prétendent souvent le contraire (avec un peu de «diplomatie» on arrive à faire parler «patois» ou au moins le comprendre à des personnes qui déclaraient quelques minutes avant n'en rien savoir!) ... Et là les chiffres montent considé-rablement. Dans la plupart des communautés rurales, on atteint sans doute presque les 100%!
>   ... Les langues locales sont en France des langues honteuses, victimes d'un syndrome diglossique aigu. On les cache, on ne les parle qu'entre initiés et l'on prétend ne pas les connaître ... Il faut ... une grande persévérance pour percer cette «stratégie de dissimulation» linguistique et culturelle (consciente ou inconsciente) ... Je connais des gens qui vivent en Provence depuis plus de trente ans et n'ont jamais entendu parler provençal, alors que je sais pertinemment que les Provençaux qui les entourent, leurs voisins, le parlent quotidiennement entre eux!
>   ... Certains criaient déjà à la fin des «patois» au début du XIXe siècle. On a ensuite déclaré que le tournant se situait entre 1880 et 1914. Puis on s'est rendu compte que les parlers locaux étaient bien vivants jusque dans les années 1930. On en est aujourd'hui à considérer que le tournant se situe vers les années 1950! Peut-être le situera-t-on vers 2010 en 2050?
>
>   (Blanchet 1994: 96–100)

Bretagne romane: Romance-speaking Brittany, i.e. the eastern region (notably the Ille-et-Vilaine department) which lies outside the Breton-speaking area. The traditional dialect here is a *langue d'oïl* variety known as *Gallo*.

■ Why does this writer place *patois* in inverted commas?

■ What two neutral alternatives to it does he use?

■■ What does he mean by the following?

- *langue honteuse*
- *syndrome diglossique aigu*
- *statégie de dissimulation*

■■ What factors make predictions about the future of dialects misleading?

Echoes of this view – as well as less 'optimistic' observations – are to be found in the following accounts of specific regional languages.

Corsican

Schématiquement, on distinguera en amont une génération . . . en voie de disparition, qui se caractérise par un monolinguisme corse et une compétence passive plus ou moins importante du français. Au bout de la chaîne, principalement dans les villes, on trouve une génération dont le français est résolument l'unique langue mater- nelle, mais un français . . . qui connaît un registre «régional» très marqué sur les plans phonétique, syntaxique et lexical. Cette généra- tion a parfois – mais non toujours – une compétence «passive» du corse qu'elle dit comprendre mais ne pas parler. On a d'ailleurs fait remarquer que le «passage à l'acte» pouvait se faire, dans cette génération, chez les hommes surtout, à l'âge adulte, comme mani- festation d'intégration à la communauté. Entre ces deux extrêmes, on trouve une génération dont le corse est la langue maternelle et le français «la langue du dimanche», c'est-à-dire une langue très soignée et très conservatrice . . . fortement marquée par un apprentissage exclusivement scolaire . . .

En relation avec les événements politiques de ces quinze dernières années, la situation sociolinguistique corse a connu une brusque évolution. On peut schématiser les choses en disant que se développe, chez certains militants politico-culturels, qui bien souvent n'avaient pas de liens avec la communauté authentiquement corso- phone, une variété de corse . . . fondée sur les caractéristiques linguistiques du français dont elle emprunte largement les traits phoniques, syntaxiques et lexicaux. Les tenants de cette variété linguistique cherchent à étendre largement son emploi, par rapport à la variété «héritée». Il s'agit de montrer que le corse, langue adulte, langue nationale du peuple corse, est capable d'assumer toutes les fonctions imparties à une langue. D'où l'élaboration de lexiques techniques, l'utilisation par les médias du corse pour commenter l'actualité internationale, une émission de jazz entremêlant corse et anglais, etc... Si on se félicite, d'une manière très générale, du regain de faveur et d'emploi que connaît le corse aujourd'hui, on est très sévère sur la manière qu'ont les nouveaux venus à l'usage de la langue de «sfrancisà», de «straccià u corsu» ...: «si c'est pour parler comme ça, je préfère qu'ils ne parlent plus corse»; «ce n'est plus notre langue», etc. Il ne s'agit pas d'une opposition de génération: un jeune homme d'une trentaine d'années, corsophone «authentique» et militant culturel, déclarait que ses camarades parlaient «comme des synthétiseurs».

(Dalbera-Stefanaggi 1991: 166)

■ In Corsica, which is the vehicular and which the vernacular language?

■ In what ways does the use of Corsican differ between the generations?

■■ Why do Corsican nationalists have mixed feelings about the current revival of the Corsican language?

Alsatian

The mixture which one finds in Strasbourg, at a cultural level, between traditional regional elements (e.g. architecture, dialect theatre, traditional bakeries, the Christmas market...) and French/international elements is...echoed by the linguistic mixture which the visitor cannot help but hear when walking around or shopping...

CONRAD: Ich bin do, morje!
RICK: Ja.
CONRAD: Y a pas de problèmes!
RICK: So Gott will, gell? Bonsoir monsieur Wanner...

The overall picture which emerges [from a 1979 study] is of about three-quarters of the adult population speaking Alsatian. This is probably still roughly accurate, with considerable variation between town and countryside, Strasbourg in particular being predominantly francophone. But although a survey of adults' use might not show much change ... the dialect is not necessarily being transmitted to the youngest generation even in families where both parents speak it ... In the country, when both parents speak Alsatian, 92.7% of their children speak it also; in town, in the same circumstances, only 70% of the children speak it – and their command of it is probably much poorer and their active use much less frequent than that of their parents. In urban families where only one of the two parents speaks Alsatian, a mere 16.8% of children speak it where that parent is the mother and 13% where it is the father.

What one can now say with some confidence [in respect of such urban environments] is that children who are actively bilingual are in a minority and the majority speak only French. On the other hand, I came across numerous signs of the children's passive knowledge of the dialect; for example, children often intervene in conversations between adults in Alsatian, usually using French themselves but showing perfect understanding of the dialect. Conversations between children and grandparents are not infrequently conducted with the children speaking French and the grandparent Alsatian, each under-standing the other perfectly but making no apparent attempt to accommodate to the other ... One has the impression – perhaps mistaken – that if one could just say the magic word to remove the inhibition, the self-imposed rule that Alsatian is an adults' language – or a vulgar language – then countless children and teenagers who never utter a word of Alsatian would suddenly start speaking it fluently ... It seems very likely ... that the dialect ... resurfaces in adolescent boys and takes on the role of an in-language in that group, symbolizing and reinforcing male solidarity.

(Gardner Chloros 1991: 2–3, 18–21, 32–3)

■■ Alsace came under French sovereignty in 1678, but was incorporated into the German Reich from 1871 until 1919 and again from 1940 until 1944. The loyalist feelings of Alsatians towards France are well-known: what effect would you expect them to have had on local language attitudes?

Occitan

Occitan is above all the language of the countryside as opposed to the town. Coherent groups of primary speakers are to be found only in rural communities, far from the main communication routes. The smaller the community, the greater the probability of finding speakers who have learnt Occitan naturally and who use it fluently ...

The domains of officialdom (administration, politics, mass media, school, church) have been dominated by French for a long time. While Occitan has won a certain place in school and literature, its importance in the mass media is virtually zero ... There are no newspapers written in Occitan. Radio and television stations allot only a few minutes to Occitan ...

Case studies so far show that Occitan is used in families, above all for communication between parents and grandparents, less for communication between the father and mother or between children and grandparents, and not at all for communication between parents and children, which is almost exclusively in French. Conversely, Occitan has a certain importance for communication in child peer-groups, where it acquires a quasi-secret, exclusive function. Outside the family Occitan is used above all for activities embedded in agricultural society (market, work in the fields and vineyards) and for men's leisure activities (café, fishing, bowls).

In my opinion, language conflict between Occitan and French is characterized by the large gap between linguistic behaviour and discourse on language(s). In hardly any other linguistic community are the differences between what is done and what is said so striking ... [People are] proud of belonging to the Occitanophone community, without speaking the language ... Even those who are convinced of the value of Occitan have little hope of revitalizing it. The process of substitution seems to have advanced too far, so that there are no remaining functions and domains of genuine Occitan use which could serve as a starting point for revitalization or normalization comparable to that in Catalonia in the last ten years.

(Schlieben-Lange 1993: 221–6)

■ Why might it be said that the current enthusiasm for Occitan language and culture has 'come too late'?

■■ What evidence can be found in these three accounts for the 'covert' knowledge of local languages referred to earlier by Blanchet (1994)?

■■ What similarities and differences can you detect between the situations of the various regional languages described? Use the following headings as a starting point:

- – Language standardized or not?
- – Spoken in how compact and uniform a geographical area?
- – Spoken by what percentage of the population?
- – Urban or rural use?
- – Used by all generations? In the same way?
- – Main circumstances of use?
- – Any links with regionalist/nationalist sentiment?

■■ How well do you think each of them is likely to have been maintained in fifty or a hundred years' time?

■■■ Present a portrait of any other regional language of France about which you can obtain information.

■■■ Do regional languages and dialects really have a place in the modern world, or are they just a barrier to communication?

Further reading

Read Lodge (1993) to find out how the French of Paris achieved its present pre-eminence. A vivid picture of the use of regional languages and dialects in nineteenth-century France is given in Chapter 6 of Weber (1979). Chapter 4 of Sanders (1993) contains information about today's regional languages. On dialects as well as languages, see also Muller (1985), Rossillon (1995) and Walter (1988).

●   ●   ●

Chapter 5

Local varieties of French in France

Français régional

Despite the marginalization of regional languages and dialects, these have had their own local influence on the standard language. The process whereby a dialect or regional language is superseded by 'standard French', or an approximation to it, involves a period of bilingualism during which both are used side by side. But there is no hard and fast dividing line between standard and dialect. For instance, in the still-extant dialect of Gondecourt (in the Nord department), *robli* corresponds to standard French *oublier*, but an intermediate form *oubli* is also heard. Similarly: *ti* (dialect), *toi* (standard), *toay* (intermediate).

■ Which of the following is the standard equivalent of 'on the sink', which is dialect and which is intermediate between the two?

su l'glacis; *sur le glacier*; *sur l'évier*

(data from Carton 1981)

In fact it is possible to recognize as many as three gradations within the non-standard forms: 'pure dialect' ↔ 'dialect with French influence' ↔ 'French with dialect influence' (↔ 'standard French'). As time passes, 'pure dialect' will be used by fewer and fewer speakers and possibly disappear altogether, 'dialect-influenced French' will become predominant over 'French-influenced dialect', and approximate increasingly to the standard, without necessarily becoming identical to it. This kind of 'French with dialect or local language influence' is commonly referred to as *français régional*.

Here are two examples of Corsican *français régional* (from Thiers 1993: 263–4):

– A middle-aged bilingual speaker:

Le dimanche je porte ma femme à sentir la musique des soldats
('On Sundays I take my wife to hear the military band')

– A young monolingual speaker of regional French:

> On a scrouqué une bagnole, et puis, en face de l'Arinella, elle a
> spatsé, spatsé . . . de peu on se charbe . . .
> ('We nicked a car, but near Arinella, it skidded about . . . and we
> nearly crashed . . . ')

Corsican *scruccà*: 'steal', *spazzà*: 'skid', *scialbassì*: 'collide'

■ What two different kinds of lexical influence of Corsican on French
are illustrated here?

■■ 'Le français régional est ce qui reste des patois lorsque ceux-ci ont
disparu.' Can you explain this statement?

Regionalisms of vocabulary and grammar

The Corsican examples above are specific to the island. In mainland
France too, there are highly localized regionalisms of vocabulary: in the
Saône-et-Loire *bologne* is the equivalent of *betterave*, and people speak of
une raie de chocolat rather than *une barre*. Some terms are used more
widely, and may even be included in standard dictionaries. Thus *fada (fou)*
is common in the south-east – the famous modernistic block of flats
built by Le Corbusier in Marseilles, for example, is known to locals as *la
maison du fada* – and this word now figures in the *Petit Larousse*. Other
terms may be used in standard French (or in other regional varieties) but
with a different meaning: in the Dijon area, *chétif* refers to a person who
is small and malevolent, not to one who is small and unhealthy, while
montagne designates any hilly and wooded area, so that *bois de haute
montagne* may come from altitudes of no more than 500m. In parts of the
south, *aboyer* and *japper* ('bark' and 'yap' respectively in standard French)
both mean 'bark', but *aboyer* is felt as belonging to a more formal level
of language, so that *japper* is the usual term. In the region of Clermont-
Ferrand (but not elsewhere) *rentrer au domaine* would be an entirely
unpretentious way of saying 'return to the farm'.

Nowadays lexical regionalisms relate above all to aspects of rural life
(as can be seen from several of the above examples) or else to local particularisms, notably gastronomic ones like *cacou* for the cherry cake which
is a speciality of Paray-le-Monial in the Saône-et-Loire, or *pauchouse* for

a fish soup from Verdun-sur-le-Doubs. (The name of a more famous fish soup, the *bouillabaisse* of Marseilles, has long ceased to be felt as regional and has passed into standard – indeed international – usage.) A few terms survive as names of fashionable restaurants: *Le Pôchon* ('ladle') near Dijon, or *L'Hutau* ('guest-room') east of Lyons. (Data mainly from Taverdet 1990: 704–16.)

■■　What aspects of modern life do you think account for this restriction of the use of regional vocabulary items?

■■　How do you suppose regionalisms are affected by the spread of standard usage and by the increasing mobility of speakers?

Grammar can also show regional features. The past historic tense, for instance, is commonly encountered in spoken usage in south-western France. Here is an account of some other examples of *régionalismes grammaticaux*.

> Lors d'une grève des transports routiers, un conducteur de poids lourd interrogé par un journaliste de télévision, sur son salaire et ses conditions de travail, a conclu sa réponse par cette phrase: «*Pour faire ce travail il faut y aimer*». Visiblement le journaliste a été surpris . . . Il s'agit d'un régionalisme grammatical, très courant . . . à l'est d'une ligne qui va d'Autun à Valence: entre trois et quatre millions de Français parlent ordinairement de cette façon, tout à fait contraire à la «grammaire» du français.
>
> 　　Voici d'autres exemples. Dans le nord de la Champagne et de la Lorraine, on emploie un sujet devant l'infinitif construit avec *pour*: «J'ai acheté de bons souliers pour moi porter cet hiver». Dans le sud-ouest de la France, la reprise d'un pronom personnel, sujet ou objet, se fait à l'aide de la préposition *à*: «Qu'est-ce qu'il a à me regarder, à moi, ce type-là?» ou bien: «S'il continue à m'agacer, je vais aller le voir, à moi!» En Dauphiné, on inverse l'ordre des pronoms personnels . . . : «Elle peut garder ma poupée, je lui la donne» . . . Une région méridionale allant au moins de Toulouse à Montpellier accorde les participes passés dans des contextes pour lesquels la grammaire officielle exige l'invariabilité: «Cette lettre, je ne l'ai plus pour le moment, je l'ai faite taper par la secrétaire» . . . De la Savoie jusqu'au Pays Basque, le verbe *être* se conjugue avec lui-même, aux temps composés: «Je suis été malade».
>
> 　　　　　　　　　　　　　　　　　　　　　　　　(Tuaillon 1988: 295–6)

- List the regionalisms mentioned, giving their standard French equivalents.

- In which *départements* are they likely to be encountered?

■■ To what extent do you think it likely that the use of regional features of grammar and vocabulary correlates with the speaker's level of education?

Pronunciation: realities and mythologies

Regional grammar or vocabulary items may well occur only sporadically in the course of actual speech, but as every word in an utterance is likely to be affected by a difference of accent, it is in pronunciation that the influence of local dialects and languages is most noticeable. Moreover, it is regional pronunciations which give rise to the most lively reactions on the part of speakers from other regions.

Wide-ranging accounts of the main accents encountered in metropolitan France are to be found in the books mentioned at the end of the chapter. Here we focus on just a few particularly well-known varieties. Sounds are indicated here by symbols of the International Phonetic Alphabet (in square brackets). A list of those relevant for French will be found in any good French–English dictionary.

The Midi and Alsace

The following sound features are well-known indicators of particular French accents, including those of southern and eastern France. They are comparable to, say, the presence or absence of *r* in words like *hard* or *car* in the English-speaking world.

1   *r*: never silent, but some accents have a front 'alveolar' [r], while others (including the standard) have a back, 'uvular' [ʀ].
2   *a*: standard French has a 'front' *a* in *tache, patte* [taʃ, pat] (similar to English *mat*), but a 'back' *a* in *tâche, pâte* [taʃ, pɑt] (more like English *mast*). But many other varieties (including some of those heard in Paris) don't follow this pattern.

3   o: the vowels of *rose* [ʀoz] and *rosse* [ʀɔs] are distinct in standard French, but identical in some accents.

4   nasal vowels: these can be key defining features of particular accents (notably the ones in words like *blanc* and *vin*).

5   *m* and *n* after nasal vowels: in standard French, in words like *bonté* or *importe*, *m* and *n* aren't pronounced as independent consonants, but they *are* pronounced in some other accents. In such accents, too, an [ŋ] (like the *ng* of English *hang*) occurs at the ends of words after a nasal vowel: in *vin*, for example.

6   'mute' *e*: (as in *bonne*, *chose*) is not always mute.

7   the so-called *h aspiré*: this is silent in standard French, though it does prevent the elision of *le* in *le héros*, and the liaison with *Les* in *Les Halles*. However it actually is an audible [h] in some accents.

8   *b, d, g*: these may be realized as *p, t, k*, and even vice versa.

■■ Using the sources recommended at the end of the chapter, and/or any native speakers who may be able to help you, fill in the gaps in Table 5.1, assigning the above features to one or other of the accents indicated.

TABLE 5.1

Feature	Midi	Alsace
r	both [r] and [ʀ] are heard, depending on the area	[r] is alveolar
a		'back' [ɑ] used
o		as standard
nasal vowels		as standard
m, n and [ŋ] after nasal vowels		
h	as standard	
'mute' *e*		
b, d, g	as standard	

■   Why are *mère* and *père* words of two syllables in the south, but only one in the north and east?

■   Explain why the author of a humorous article about the Midi in *Le Canard Enchaîné* represents the place-name *Tourcoing* as

Tourcoingue, and *la chemise blanche de Madame Rose* as *la chemiseu blancheu de Madameu Roseu*.

■■ The regional French of the Midi is by no means uniform. Marseillais and Toulousain accents are differentiated by *r*, among other things. Can you specify how?

■ It is part of French folklore that Alsatians are unable to tell the difference between a glass of claret (*bordeaux*) and a glass of port (*porto*). What is the basis for this assumption?

■■ The same feature of Alsatian accents has given rise to riddles such as:

Mon premier est une lettre grecque; mon deuxième est un poisson; mon troisième est sur le toit; mon entier se trouve dans chaque garage d'Alsace.

The answer is: *bidon d'huile*. Can you explain this by reference to the Alsatian pronunciation of the phrase?

The *accent du Midi*, too, is celebrated enough to have its own mythology. For instance, it is often described as being 'un accent chantant'. In a study designed to find out whether southern pronunciation does have particularly musical qualities (and, if so, exactly what these might be), subjects with no knowledge of French whatsoever (they were from Wales in fact) were asked to listen to voices of speakers from northern and southern France and to give a personal impression of their accents. These impressions were then compared with instrumental measurements of speed (*débit*), intonation (*structure mélodique*) and rhythm, and the following conclusions emerged:

Les résultats tendent à prouver qu'on ne peut établir aucune corrélation entre des faits phonétiques d'accent régional et un certain «type» anthropologique, physique ou caractériel. On a pourtant décelé une distinction: le groupe méridional fut jugé «le plus vif» ... Il ne s'agit pas du débit: l'analyse ... du débit moyen de chaque locuteur a montré que trois des cinq échantillons du français du Nord indiquaient un débit plus rapide que pour le français du Midi. La comparaison des structures mélodiques n'a rien donné de significatif non plus. En revanche les structures temporelles des méridionaux manifestaient une plus grande irrégularité des syllabes non accentués. Cette différence de «pattern» rythmique a pu donner une impression de vivacité.

(Carton 1987: 37–8)

■ Summarize the results of this study, and say what they suggest about the objective reality of the *accent chantant du Midi*.

■■ Make your own enquiries among native francophones in order to find out whether they too share the belief.

Paris and the north

North of the Loire, Parisian accents have become dominant. Standard French (in origin the pronunciation of the Paris aristocracy and bourgeoisie) has supplanted local pronunciations among the middle classes to a far greater extent than in the south or in Alsace. Likewise, in urban centres such as Rouen, Le Havre, Caen or Rennes, the local working-class or 'popular' accent is indistinguishable from its Parisian counterpart. (However, in the Lille region a variety of pronunciation is encountered which has many affinities with accents heard in neighbouring Belgium – see Chapter 6.)

■■ What historical and geographical factors explain why these basically Parisian features are so widespread across northern France?

The following features are characteristic of the *accent populaire parisien*, *accent faubourien*, or *accent de banlieue*, as it is also called.

1   [ɑ] replaced by [a], so that the pronunciation of *tâche* becomes identical to that of *tache* : [taʃ].
2   [ɛ̃] for standard [œ̃], e.g. *brun* and *brin* are both pronounced [bʀɛ̃]
3   Tendency to omit [ə] in phrases like *nous retrouvons* (*r'trouvons*) [nuʀtʀuvɔ̃] or *beaucoup de peine* (*d'peine*) [bokudpɛn]
4   Converse tendency to insert [ə] into groups of three or more consonants, e.g. Félix Potin [feliksəpɔtɛ̃], *Arc de Triomphe* [aʀkədətʀiɔ̃f] (*Félix-eu-Potin, arqueu-de-triomphe*).
5   [œ] or [ø] for standard [ɔ], e.g. in *joli* (sometimes represented by novelists as *jeuli*), and for standard [ə], e.g. in *vendredi* (*vendreudi*)
6   [ɛʀ] for standard [aʀ], e.g. in *soir* (*souère*) [swɛʀ]

7   weakening of *v* between vowels, e.g. in *avec* (*a'ec*) [aɛk]

■   Which of these features would account for such spelling errors as
     Beaujelais for *Beaujolais*, and why?

Over the last hundred years or so, features (1), (2) and (3) in particular
have become more and more widely encountered in urban middle-class
speech also. In the late nineteenth century, observations like the following
were already being made (this one is from a guide to good diction entitled
L'Art de bien dire):

> Que de gens disent: *ôkin, kelkin, chakin, in* pour *aucun, quelqu'un,
> chacun, un*. C'est une faute déplorable contre laquelle on ne se
> tiendra jamais trop en garde.
>
> (quoted in Nève de Mévergnies 1984: 199)

■   Specify the ongoing change in pronunciation which this commentator
     so disapproves of.

By 1968, although State radio announcers and newsreaders adhered to
traditional conventions by continuing to pronounce *emprunte* and
empreinte differently ([ɑ̃pʀœ̃t] and [ɑ̃pʀɛ̃t]), this was not the case with
their counterparts on the more 'trendy' commercial stations like RTL or
Europe 1, only 50 per cent of whom were making such distinctions.
According to a study made at the time, one speaker's view was that:

> [œ̃] fait *enfant sage*; [ɛ̃] manifeste beaucoup plus *d'attaque* et de
> *mordant*.

And the investigator reports (ibid.: 212):

> ... [vers 1968] des amis parisiens, devant qui j'articulais conscien-
> cieusement le [œ̃] pour qu'ils l'entendent, se récriaient: Ça! un son
> français?

■■   What do such findings and reactions suggest about the way changes
     in pronunciation tend to be accompanied by changes in people's
     attitudes to particular sounds?

Here is some further evidence of speakers' lack of awareness of ongoing
change. Feature (3) – the tendency to omit [ə] – is a favourite stereotype

for writers aiming to reproduce the speech of working-class Parisians. An example follows from a novel set in a *quartier populaire* near Montmartre.

> Son instinct le conduisit devant un restaurant pour touristes. Il lut le menu. «Pas d'plats à moins d'quatre cents balles. Ah! si, dans les hors-d'oeuvre, la terrine à trois cents balles. Trois cents balles, j'ferais trois repas avec ça! Et y'a des gars qui prennent de tous les plats. Avec le service et tout l'reste, y z'en ont au moins pour deux sacs. Et y z'amènent leurs poules. Là d'dans, avant d'bouffer t'en as déjà pour trois cents balles de serviette, de couvert et tout l'tremblement . . . »
>
> (Sabatier 1956: 233–4)

Yet long before this was written, a distinguished analyst of colloquial French was already commenting as follows on such spelling conventions:

> . . . nous avons une tradition qui veut qu'on remplace dans le dialogue populaire les «e» muets par des apostrophes. Prenons, par exemple, le titre d'un article [de] journal. Il s'agissait d'un ex-coureur cycliste qui avait fait un numéro sur une scène de music-hall. On lui fait dire (c'est cela qui fournit le titre, en gros caractères): *L'théâtre, moi, ça m'plaît!* Qu'y a-t-il de populaire là-dedans? Nous entendrons très bien l'homme cultivé dire: «L'théâtre, moi, ça m'fatigue.» (Et même: «L'théât'».) La plupart des romanciers abusent des apostrophes dans leurs dialogues populaires et argotiques . . . Si on écrivait *maint'nant, tranquill'ment, él'vait,* on . . . écrirait . . . le français comme il se parle à Paris dans toutes les classes de la société . . . Et aussi *ç'keu ça peu ét' bête* pour «ce que ça peut être bête». Tous les Parisiens prononcent [cette dernière phrase] de la même façon, pour peu qu'elle soit dite dans le mouvement, avec conviction et naturellement.
>
> (Bauche 1928: 158)

- What misconception is being criticized here?

- What are the sociological facts about the omission of 'mute *e*'?

■■ In the excerpt from Sabatier's novel above, can you find one or two other purportedly working-class Parisian features that in reality are used by francophones from all kinds of different backgrounds?

■■ What do such attempts at transcription, together with Henri Bauche's comments, suggest about the perceptions middle-class Parisians have concerning their pronunciation?

Touraine (the 'best' pronunciation)

Although standard French originated in Paris, there is a widespread belief that the 'best French' is spoken in the Loire Valley, around Tours and Orléans. This idea goes back several centuries and has even found its way into the guidebooks. Thus the *Insight Guide to France* comments:

> ... the Val de Loire has welcomed little foreign influence over the centuries. Red-cheeked winegrowers and well-heeled housewives alike speak the purest French.

That the 'pure French of Touraine' is in fact about as real as the 'accent chantant du Midi', emerges from research by Nicole Gueunier (see also the discussion in Sanders 1993: 75–6). Comments like the following were collected from inhabitants of various localities within the Indre-et-Loire department (the Touraine district proper; see Map 5.1). All the comments related either to their own French or to the French heard in neighbouring villages (quotations from Gueunier 1991: 42–50).

On parle un assez bon français, on n'a pas d'accent.

Ils parlent drôlement.

Ils causent en traînant.

On parle plus dur, plus fort, plus grave, on écorche les mots. Les Parisiens ne nous comprennent pas parce qu'on avale les mots.

A Bourgueil, ils causent mieux que nous, c'est plus grandiose ... Ceux qui sont dans les champs, ça n'est pas le même causement que ceux qui sont en ville ou dans le bourg.

Ceux qui sont sortis des bois, du fond des prés, vous pouvez toujours y aller ... «Rhabiller les chaussettes», c'est «raccommoder». «Rhabiller», c'est pour les vieux, moi, j'ai jamais dit ça! Et y en a qui le disent encore, qui sont plus jeunes que moi: mais alors ils sont dans les bois!

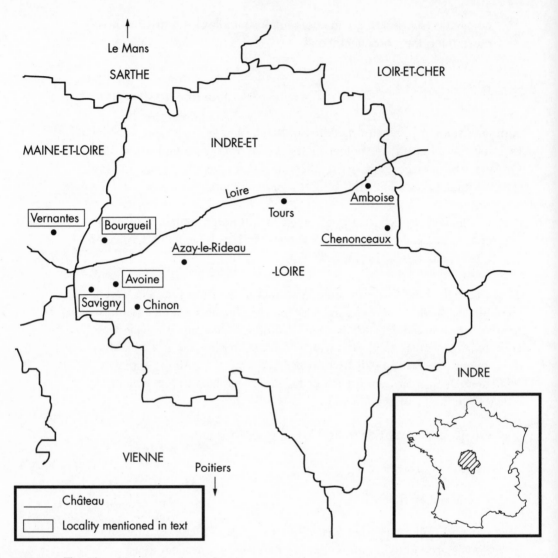

MAP 5.1 Touraine

Sur Savigny, y a une ponctuation plus prononcée que dans les autres communes, y a un patois . . .

Nous, on parle mal, très mal, mais à Savigny . . . c'est encore plus mal que nous.

Opinions are not just about language:

A Savigny, c'est réputé un peu en retard, ils vivent chez eux, ils ne sont pas si allants qu'à Avoine, où il y a des commerces, le confort, le chauffage, des tracteurs.

Still more severe criticism is reserved for those in adjacent departments, even in localities only a few kilometres from the boundary:

Ici, on aurait peut-être tendance à rouler les *r* mais c'est pas comme dans le Maine-et-Loire.

. . . les Sarthois, j'aime pas leur façon de parler. Ils naissent avec ça. Ça fait paysan.

Dans la Sarthe . . . faut voir leur charabia!

Du côté de Vernantes ils ne causent pas comme nous.

Some informants held quite surprising beliefs about the ethnic origins of their near neighbours. The allusion in the following is to the battle of Poitiers in AD732, and the victory of Charles Martel over the advancing Islamic army:

On n'a pas de patois, vraiment pas. La Touraine a échappé à tous les envahisseurs et à toutes les pollutions, comparativement à d'autres pays . . . Les Arabes étaient venus jusqu'à Poitiers . . . Ça a laissé quelques traces de gens qui sont restés bon teint depuis le temps, qui ont un type quelque peu arabe . . . Ici, on est Tourangeaux pure race!

Not everyone in Touraine would agree with the last statement, for another informant commented:

Les gens de Savigny, ce sont des Bédouins, ils sont bruns, ils ont les yeux noirs, la peau basanée, les femmes vêtues de couleurs voyantes, grands travailleurs.

- How many non-standard features of grammar or vocabulary can you detect in these comments by speakers of allegedly 'pure French'?

- ■ What do their observations suggest about the idea that a uniformly correct or standard French is spoken everywhere in the Loire Valley?

■■ What insight do they give into speakers' views of their neighbours and their speech-habits?

One interviewee offered the following explanation for the belief about the superiority of Touraine French. Evidently she had in mind the royal châteaux that are a feature of the Loire Valley.

En Touraine, on parle le mieux français, c'est reconnu, même en Belgique. C'est peut-être parce qu'on a eu des rois autrefois, habitant notre province.

■■ Why might this suggest that the type of French spoken by people from Touraine depends as much on social class as it does on regional origins?

Attitudes, stereotypes and linguistic insecurity

As some of the above material suggests, regional usage – and pronunciation in particular – can trigger off strong reactions. Here are some responses collected from a group of thirty middle-class speakers (from various regions) who were asked to evaluate recordings of *alsacien*, *méridional* (southern), popular Parisian and standard pronunciations.

Informants were first asked whether they liked the accent in question.

Alsatian (Strasbourg)	yes 9	neutral 10	no 11
Southern (Marseilles)	yes 25	neutral 3	no 2
Popular Parisian	yes 2	neutral 10	no 18
Standard	yes 16	neutral 10	no 4

Some of their reasons were established:

Alsatian	['yes' answers] folklorique, sympathie pour la région
	['no' answers] dur, hâché, laid, allemand, pas harmonieux
Southern	['yes'] chantant, chaud, ensoleillé, sympathique, musical, pittoresque, j'aime le sud
Parisian	['no'] traînant, vulgaire, pas harmonieux
Standard	['yes'] correct, expressif, harmonieux, cultivé, vivant

Next they were asked whether they would correct their child if he or she were heard speaking with an accent:

Alsatian	yes 18	no 11	no answer/undecided	1
Southern	yes 8	no 17	no answer/undecided	5
Parisian	yes 20	no 10	no answer/undecided	0
Standard	yes 8	no 20	no answer/undecided	2

Again, reasons were sought:

Alsatian ['yes' answers] trop particulariste, pas français, peut lui nuire plus tard, trahit un manque d'instruction
['no' answers] normal pour la région, me plaît

Southern ['yes'] trop fort
['no'] normal pour la région, accent agréable, n'est pas une barrière sociale

Parisian ['yes'] vulgaire, mauvais, laid, barrière sociale
['no'] on ne peut jamais rien faire contre cette façon de parler, l'accent n'est pas important

Standard ['yes'] affecté, pas naturel
['no'] correct, brillant

Informants were also asked to imagine the personalities behind the recorded voices:

Alsatian raide, timide, réservé, discipliné, sérieux, gauche, modeste, type germanique

Southern vif, bonhomme assuré, amusant, relaxé, a quelque chose de proxénète, Marius sur la Canebière buvant son pastis

Parisian poseur, palabreur, un peu 'm'as-tu vu?', traîne dans les cafés, pressé, sûr de lui, décontracté

Standard élégant, distingué, assuré, digne, cultivé, a l'habitude de parler en public

When asked to guess the levels of education corresponding to the different voices, 85 per cent of informants judged the speaker with the standard accent to have a university degree. But no more than 9 per cent estimated the speakers with other accents to have reached this level. In fact, 41 per cent reckoned the Alsatian to have no educational qualifications at all, and 12 per cent took the same view of the popular Parisian speaker. When asked what might be the favourite reading matter of the speakers, one respondent went so far as to suggest *Mein Kampf* for the Alsatians! (data from Hoppe 1976).

- Which accents are most positively regarded and which most negatively?

- What stereotypes of the accents and their users emerge from these responses?

■■ Do the reactions (and therefore the accents themselves) carry implications about social class or educational level?

■■ Are the evaluations totally consistent?

■■ What factors might give rise to the stereotypes (memories of holidays, historical events, plays or films, etc.)?

It is not necessarily the case that speakers have unfavourable views only of the accents of those from other regions or social classes. Here are some views emerging from a survey in which speakers were asked what they thought about their *own* pronunciation. This investigation was conducted among various inhabitants of Le Havre who speak with an accent of the 'popular Parisian' kind (in some cases, despite attempts to get rid of it). This accent is widely believed by the Havrais to be specific to their town, though it is doubtful whether a distinct urban *accent du Havre* really exists.

1 *Shipping clerk*: C'est un accent qui a du charme, comme tous les accents.
2 *Law student*: C'est pas un bel accent. Les mecs se foutaient de ma gueule.
3 *Docker*: C'est un accent qu'est pas pire qu'ailleurs. Moi, je suis fier de mon accent. Quand je vais en vacances quelque part, on me dit que j'ai un accent. C'est plutôt bien.
4 *Business student*: C'est un accent affreux, vulgaire. C'est un accent de marchand de braille.
5 *Professional musician*: C'est un accent de branleur. Quand j'allais à Evreux ou même à Paris pour mes études, on me disait «vous, vous venez du Havre». J'ai toujours essayé de m'en débarasser.
6 *Loading supervisor*: Bof! C'est pas très chantant, c'est un peu gouailleur, mais bon . . .

7   *Student of English*: C'est pas un bel accent. C'est même détestable.

(data from Hauchecorne 1996)

■   Classify these statements into those where the *auto-stereotype* (speaker's view of his or her own usage) is favourable or neutral and those where it is not.

■■   How far do these speakers' occupations explain the presence or absence of feelings of insecurity about their pronunciation?

■■■ Make enquiries among native francophones of your acquaintance in order to establish their attitudes towards different regional usages – and towards their own variety of French.

■■■ Are regional variations a sign of welcome diversity or – given the negative attitudes sometimes encountered – simply an obstacle to social harmony and to the social advancement of individuals?

Further reading

There is plenty of material on regional usage in France in Chapter 3 of Sanders (1993). See also Muller (1985) and Walter (1988). Carton (1983) provides an audiocassette containing recordings of the main regional accents, together with a detailed handbook.

●   ●   ●

Chapter 6

Local varieties of French outside France

Europe: Belgium and the *Suisse romande*

Regional variation of the kind discussed in Chapter 5 is not, of course, confined to metropolitan France: other parts of francophone Europe have their own distinctive features of pronunciation, grammar and vocabulary. Obviously individuals vary in the extent to which their French has local particularities, but those referred to here are quite widespread.

Pronunciation

First, it should be noted that Walloon and Romand accents have certain characteristics in common (Bovet 1988: 12; Pohl 1985: 14–15).

1   The *a* of *pâte* and *tâche* is longer than the *a* of *patte* and *tache*.
2   There is a contrast between 'open' and 'close' *e* in pairs like *piqué* [pike] versus *piquet* [pikɛ], *et* [e] versus *est* [ɛ] ([e] as in *bébé*; [ɛ] as in *bête*).
3   There are four nasal vowels (the ones exemplified in *un bon vin blanc*). The features of nasal vowels characteristic of southern France are not encountered. At the same time the vowels of *brun* and *brin* are kept distinct by the majority of speakers, whereas in northern France this is often not the case.
4   The vowel of *née* is longer in duration [ne:] than that of *né* [ne]; similarly with other feminine/masculine pairs.
5   Words like *scier*, *lion* or *louer* consist of two syllables not one: *sci-er*, *li-on*, *lou-er* (not [sje], [ljɔ̃], [lwe].
6   As in northern (as opposed to southern) France, 'mute *e*' really is silent in *une bonne chose*, etc.

■   How many syllables would there consequently be in *social*?

■   Use the following sentence (Pohl 1985) to illustrate each of the above points:

L'ourse brun pâle est enrouée.

Some of these features are shared with the more conservative metropolitan pronunciations: in France the differentiation between long and short vowels was common in the nineteenth century, and the pronunciation of *lundi* as *lindi* is still frowned upon, though it is very widespread north of the Loire.

■■ What historical, geographical or political reasons might there be for the relative conservatism of Belgian and Swiss pronunciations?

In addition to these shared characteristics, there are, of course, a number of specifically Swiss or Belgian features.

In Switzerland a distinction is made between the *-eau* of *peau* or *artichaut* and the *-o-* of *pot* or *abricot* – the latter being pronounced like the [ɔ] of standard Fr *bonne*. Swiss speakers have a tendency to accentuate the penultimate syllable of words, and to adopt a slower speed of delivery.

In Belgium, *huit*, *puis*, etc. are normally pronounced [wit], [pwi] (*ouit, pouis*). Many speakers replace the vowel *i* in words like *magique* or *articuler* with one resembling the vowel of English *hit*, rather than the one of *heat* ([ɪ] not [i]). They are also likely to make voiced consonants voiceless at the end of a word: *chômage* with [ʃ] not [ʒ] (*chômache*), *période* with [t] not [d].

■ This last feature would make each of the following coalesce with another word. Which?

douze   perde   marge

Many of these characteristics are found also in regions of metropolitan France adjacent to the Belgian or Swiss frontiers.

■ Which French regions and departments specifically would you expect this to apply to? Check your answer by reference to the accounts of metropolitan French pronunciation in Carton (1983) or Sanders (1993).

■■ Why are the present-day international borders not a barrier to features of pronunciation?

Grammar

Here are some sentences containing grammatical features characteristic of the *Suisse romande*:

> *Ça veut mal finir.* (It'll turn out badly.)
>
> *Il me copie dessus.* (He's copying off me.)
>
> *Le chien m'est venu contre.* (The dog came at me.)
>
> *Il faut lui aider.*
>
> *J'ai personne vu.*
>
> *On peut ça faire.*
>
> *J'ai déjà eu fait du vélo.*

- Supply standard French equivalents in each case.

Many features of this kind have been attributed to the influence of German, even though the region is solidly francophone. A view more widely accepted these days is that they have long been independent characteristics of the local *franco-provençal* dialects.

- Can you say which of the above sentences could conceivably be German-influenced, and in what way?

- Why do you think many commentators find this hypothesis implausible?

Next are some examples of grammatical features common in Belgian usage:

> *Il est trop petit que pour ouvrir la fenêtre.*
>
> *Au plus j'y pense, au plus je m'étonne.*
>
> *Qu'est-ce que c'est pour une fleur?*
>
> *J'ai eu difficile de faire ce travail.*

- Again, find standard equivalents.

Vocabulary

The following lexical variants are typical of usage in Belgium and/or Switzerland. (B) here indicates *belgicismes* and (H) *helvétismes*. Remember, however, that such regionalisms account for no larger a percentage of the total Belgian or Swiss-French vocabulary than do Anglo/American differences like *pavement/sidewalk* in English.

athénée (B)	panosse (H)
bourgeoisie (H)	poutser (H)
bourgmestre (B)	régent (B)
échevin (B)	se méconduire (B)
huitante (H)	septante (B, H)
kot (B)	sous-tasse (B, H)
maturité (H)	syndic (H)
nonante (B, H)	

Only a few of these were included in the *Petit Larousse Illustré* and the *Petit Robert* of thirty years ago. Nowadays, however, thanks to the impact of the francophone movement, dictionaries are much more hospitable to non-metropolitan items, and all the above figure in the most recent editions of these two works of reference.

■ Using dictionaries if necessary, match the *belgicismes* or *helvétismes* with their standard equivalents or definitions, namely (in random order):

fait d'être citoyen d'une commune	*quatre-vingt-dix*
maire (two occurrences)	*soixante-dix*
soucoupe	*serpillière* ('floorcloth')
certificat de fin d'études	*adjoint au maire*
professeur de collège	*quatre-vingts*
lycée	*se comporter mal*
nettoyer	*chambre d'étudiant*

■ Among these are one or two which, unlike the Swiss grammatical features given earlier, are indisputably of Germanic origin. Can you identify them?

Some regional words or expressions refer to official institutions which may be specific to the country in question, and therefore are not used outside its borders. In such cases, the political frontier acts as an absolute barrier. Such items are sometimes known as *statalismes* (words unique to a particular state).

■   What *statalismes* can you find in the above list?

The pronunciation of r in the 'Black Country': a case-study in variation

Belgian and Swiss pronunciation is far from being uniform, although local particularisms are gradually being submerged by the rising tide of standardization. Partly because of this danger, they often give rise to considerable loyalty and affection. A case in point is the variety of French characteristic of the Borinage, a former coalmining region which forms part of the *pays noir* of southern Belgium (see Map 6.1). Like the various cradles of the Industrial Revolution in Britain, this once productive and prosperous area has undergone large-scale economic decline in recent years, and the province of Hainaut now counts among the 'problem regions' of the EU. This fate, however, has not yet eradicated the traditional sense of a close-knit community, and the local pronunciation of French – the last vestige of the Walloon dialect once used in these parts – is very much bound up with this sense of distinctive identity, as is shown in a recent study (Thiam 1995).

This focuses on a single phonetic feature – *r* – and examines the way in which its use varies from one speaker to another (and even in the usage of the same individual) in some of the mining villages. In the mining villages of the Borinage, the alveolar or 'front' [r] is a traditional feature of the local *français régional*, and is still widely encountered, though nowadays it co-exists with the uvular or 'back' [ʀ] characteristic of nearby Mons and other parts of Wallonia. The way the two *r*-sounds are distributed among the members of the speech community is quite complex – age, sex and educational level being important factors – but a coherent overall pattern emerges, as can be seen from Tables 6.1 and 6.2.

The figure under [ʀ] and [r] indicates the percentage of the particular group using the sound in question; [ʀ±] relates to individuals who sometimes use one variant, sometimes the other. A 'Higher' educational level

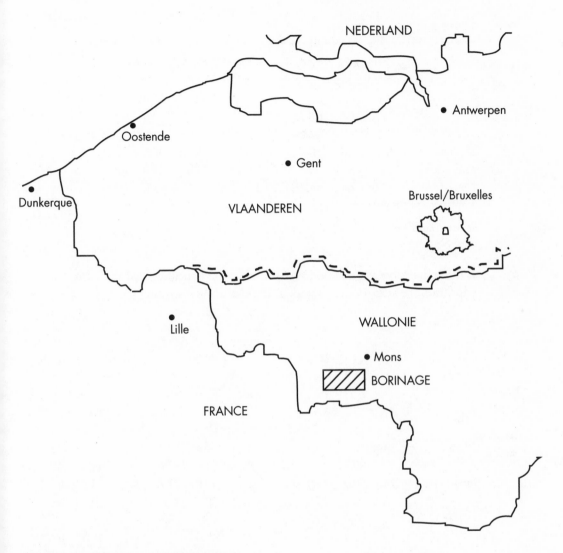

MAP 6.1 Brussels, Mons and the Borinage

implies a complete secondary and sometimes also a university education; the 'Intermediate' level corresponds to a secondary education of four years' duration; those in the 'Lower' level left secondary school without obtaining a leaving certificate.

■ Nine categories of speaker are included here. Specify which kind of r predominates in each category, and say what patterns emerge.

TABLE 6.1

	18–25 yrs			30–50 yrs			over 55 yrs		
	R (%)	r (%)	R ± (%)	R	r	R ±	R	r	R ±
Higher	60.0	40.0	0	70.0	21.9	8.1	36.3	57.7	5.9
Intermediate	60.4	33.8	5.7	44.7	43.8	11.4	29.1	61.7	9.1
Lower	30.0	65.2	4.7	20.0	75.2	4.7	25.0	75.0	0

Source: Thiam 1995

If differences between male (M) and female (F) speakers for each age and educational category are included, the picture is as follows:

TABLE 6.2

		18–25 years			30–50 years			over 55 years		
		R	r (%)	R ±	R	r (%)	R ±	R	r (%)	R ±
Higher	M	40.0	60.0	0	60.0	32.4	7.6	21.4	75.0	3.6
	F	80.0	20.0	0	80.0	11.4	8.6	51.2	40.5	8.3
Intermediate	M	60.0	40.0	0	29.5	59.0	11.4	14.3	73.3	6.1
	F	60.9	27.6	11.4	60.0	28.6	11.4	44.0	50.0	5.9
Lower	M	20.0	80.0	0	0	90.5	9.5	25.0	75.0	0
	F	40.0	50.5	9.5	40.0	60.0	0	25.0	75.0	0

In many speech communities it has been found that female speakers conform more closely to the standard than male speakers, irrespective of socioeconomic background.

■   Is this borne out by these results from the Borinage?

It also emerged that speakers in the [R±] column in Table 6.2, who are observed to use both kinds of *r*, were likely to use [R] when reading a text but switched to [r] when speaking spontaneously, especially if the topic was one in which they felt personally involved (e.g. the economic future of their region). [r] predominated with 'unstable' male speakers, but [ʀ] with females.

■■ In what way does the usage of these speakers reflect that of speakers with a more stable pronunciation?

The highest proportion of unstable [ʀ±]-users is among younger speakers in the Intermediate educational group.

■■ Why should this group be the most prone to fluctuation?

By giving a kind of snapshot of a change in progress, *variationist* studies like this one show in considerable detail how a speech community gradually changes its pronunciation, with the speech of different sections of the community evolving at different rates.

■■ What seem to be the main social factors involved in the standard-ization of the Borinage accent?

From conversations with local people, it became clear that strong associations exist between the use of local pronunciations – specifically [r] as opposed to [ʀ] – and perceptions of an [r]-user as a *'vrai Borain'*, characterized by being *'travailleur, ouvrier, mineur'* and possessing such qualities as *'générosité, jovialité, exubérance, courage, franchise'*. Thus one local politican came in for particularly favourable comment because, by continuing to use [r], he was perceived as showing solidarity with the local community. The investigator comments:

> L'usage du langage non-standard chez un grand nombre de locuteurs borains ... relève de la stratégie identitaire tendant à affirmer les valeurs prolétariennes du Borain par distinction à celles des autres, des Montois qui sont leur plus proches voisins en particulier.
> (Thiam 1995: 91–2)

Montois: inhabitant of Mons.

■■ Relate these remarks to the fact that many of the Borains questioned claimed to use [r] more frequently than they in fact did, while at the same time being rather derogatory about this pronunciation feature.

What does this suggest about their attitudes (positive or negative) towards standard and non-standard forms?

■■ *Covert prestige* is often said to attach to local speech-forms like the [r] of the Borinage. Can you explain this concept, and suggest why men are commonly more prone than women to find certain non-standard pronunciations 'prestigious'?

■■ This investigation is a good example of a variationist study. Can you attempt an explanation of this term?

North America: Quebec

Across the Atlantic, over the last three centuries, a regional French has developed that is probably even more distinctive than the varieties found outside France in Europe.

Pronunciation

The original seventeenth-century settlers in Quebec were mostly from the north-western provinces of France (Brittany, Anjou, Vendée, Loire Valley, Ile-de-France) and this accounts for the fact that Quebec pronunciation reflects northern not southern French (*langue d'oïl* not *langue d'oc*). The following regional features are found in the speech of all social classes. (The sounds are indicated here by symbols of the International Phonetic Alphabet and in certain cases also by the kind of modified spelling sometimes used for dialogue in novels.)

1   [t] and [d] with an 'affricated' pronunciation – [ts] and [dz] respectively: *lundi: lundzi* [lœ̃dzi], *constitution: constsitsution* [kɔ̃stsitsysjɔ̃]. This happens *only* before the vowels *i* and *u* ([i] and [y]): no-one would ever say *patsate* for *patate* or *bontsé* for *bonté*.
2   As is often the case in Belgium, *magique* and *politique* have [ɪ], not [i] (cf. English *sit* as opposed to *seat*). No really suitable vowel is available in ordinary French spelling, but some writers press *é* into service as an approximation (*magéque, polétséque*). [maʒɪk], [pɔlɪtsɪk] in the IPA.

3   Vowels in words like *même* or *monde* are lengthened and turned into diphthongs: [maːɪm] (or *maême*, in modified spelling), [mɔːũd] (or *moônde*).

4   The back [ɑ̃] of standard *pendant* is 'fronted' so that it approximates to that of standard French *vin*: [pãdã] (*pindint*). This resembles the southern French pronunciation, admittedly, but an important difference is that there is no [n] or [ŋ] following the vowel.

5   [ɑ] rather than [a] in words like *cassé*: [kɑse] (*câssé*).

Such features are widely accepted nowadays, though they would not have been a generation ago:

> Durant les années 60 les Québécois et en particulier ceux qui œuvraient dans les organismes de diffusion de la norme (Office de la langue française, écoles, médias) estimaient que la quasi-totalité des traits distinctifs du français québécois étaient des erreurs à déraciner et ils préconisaient un alignement complet sur le français standard dit international, voire le français hexagonal. A l'heure actuelle, on peut observer un renversement de cette tendance puisque ces mêmes organismes [affirment] que c'est le français des couches éduquées de la communauté québécoise (variété de français qui n'est pas exempte de particularismes) qui devrait être la norme de référence.
>
> (Mougeon 1994: 42–3)

■■   What social and political developments underlie this change of attitude?

Some Quebec particularisms continue to be stigmatized none the less, and have markedly working-class associations. In particular they are characteristic of the celebrated urban colloquial known as *joual* (itself named after the local pronunciation of *cheval*).

6   [wɛ] for [wa] in *moi*, etc.: [mwɛ] (*moé*)

7   [ɔ] for [a] in *mardi*, etc.: [mɔrdzi] (*mordzi*)

8   [r] instead of the more highly valued [ʀ] (*rr*)

9   Contractions like [sa] (*s'a*) for *sur la*, [ʒezevy] (*j'es ai vus*) for *je les ai vus*, [uskə] (*où c'que*) for *où est-ce que*.

■■   Here, arranged in order from most to least acceptable, are three sentences in IPA transcription and in standard spelling. Can you rewrite them in 'modified spelling', highlighting the specifically *québécois* features?

– i fɔ̃ yn bɔn kwizɪn lə samdzi swaːʀ
ils font une bonne cuisine le samedi soir.

– se tʀɛ dzɪfsɪl a fɛʀ sɛt sous lɔ
c'est très difficile à faire cette sauce-là.

– ʃfɪni mɛrkrœdi swɛr ʒvɔ kɔmãse mɔrdzi paskə lœ̃dzi se la fait lɔ lœ̃dzi prɔʃɛ̃
je finis mercredi soir, je vais commencer mardi parce que lundi c'est la fête là, lundi prochain.

(data from Lappin 1982)

■■ Identify the following items and say which of them would be acceptable in terms of the Quebec norm which appears to be emerging.

[ʀutsɪn]   [səpãdã]
[aʀtsɪkylasjɔ̃]   [swɛf]
[ãtɑse]   [pətsɪt]
[ʒatruv]   [pɔrtsi]
[dzi dɔ̃k]   [baːɪt]

(As a clue, here are the English equivalents of the four least obvious items, in order of their occurrence: *to pile up, I find it, part, silly*)

■■ After Quebec (New France as it was originally called) became a British colony in 1763, contacts with France were very much reduced and became virtually non-existent after the French Revolution of 1789. They were re-established only in the mid-twentieth century. How might this account for the existence in Canada of a much more divergent variety of pronunciation than is commonly found in Belgium or Switzerland?

Vocabulary

As with *belgicismes* and *helvétismes*, even the highly distinctive regionalisms found in the French of Quebec are a relatively minor component of the total vocabulary. *Québécismes* fall into the following main categories:

– Words now archaic or dialectal in European French:

à coup ('tout à coup'); *icitte* ('ici'); *mal-en-train* ('souffrant')

– Items coined in Canada which have no single-word equivalents in European French:

poudrerie ('neige poudreuse'); *tabagie* ('bureau de tabac')

– *Sacres* (swear words): a unique repertoire of blasphemies has evolved, including:

hostie! tabernacle! baptême! (plus related euphemisms like *baleine!*)

– 'Anti-anglicisms' (French words used in cases where European French borrows from English):

fin de semaine ('weekend'); *magasinage* ('shopping'); *traversier* ('car ferry'); *chien chaud* ('hot dog')

– Overt anglicisms:

c'est le fun ('c'est amusant'); *défroster* ('dégivrer')

– Covert anglicisms:

pour des raisons hors de notre contrôle ('pour des raisons indépendantes de notre volonté'); *voyagez sans trouble et sans fatigue* ('. . . sans ennuis . . . '); *char* ('voiture')

■ What, judging from the examples given, is the difference between an overt and a covert anglicism?

■ Which of these categories do the following belong to?

stationnement ('parking'); *chéquer* ('*vérifier*'); *berlander* ('*flâner*'); *tout le monde change* ('all change')

■ Identify specifically *québécois* features in the following:

Ah le maudit Christ! J'ai échappé ma cigarette sur le tapis!
C'est un Christ de beau char!
Hostie, t'as-tu ta carte toé pour rentrer, pour passer icitte à l'hôpital?

■■ What historical, geographical, cultural and religious features are reflected in these regional Quebec vocabulary items?

Regional French in Africa

Though only a second language in 'francophone Africa', French has developed distinctively regional characteristics through use alongside local languages, often by speakers whose knowledge of it is rudimentary. In general outline, the patterns of language interpenetration are similar to the ones found in metropolitan France:

local language(s) ↔ local language + French elements ↔ French + local elements ↔ standard French

Two important differences are, first, that vernacular and vehicular African languages (unlike most metropolitan dialects) are in no way threatened with extinction, and, second, that the extension of competence in French is unlikely to keep pace with the increase in population. So varieties like the following can be expected to go on co-existing for a long time to come.

(a) These utterances illustrate a blend of French and Wolof encountered in Senegal, which has many parallels elsewhere in West and Central Africa. Derogatory terms like *sabir franco-africain, petit-nègre*, or *petit français* are often applied, even by professional linguists.

Madame bi toujours daf may gronder su ma tarder-ee

Wolof items: *bi* = the; *daf* = she; *may* = me; *su* = if; *ma* = I; *-ee* = conditional. *Madame* here has the sense of 'schoolteacher'.

Suma papa aéroport lay liggéeye, transitaire lay def

suma = my; *lay* = he; *liggéeye* = work; *def* = do.

(data from Thiam 1994)

■ What do the sentences mean?

■ Would you say they were basically French or basically Wolof?

(b) In urban centres particularly, other *mixed codes* have developed in which the grammatical basis comes from French rather from a local language. The following dialogue from a cartoon strip illustrates the *français populaire ivoirien* (FPI) spoken in Abidjan, the principal city of Ivory Coast.

(A showman invites passers-by to try their skill at weightlifting)

– Participez au grand jeu du Café Ivoire! Vous pouvez gagner 10 000 F en essayant de soulever ces haltères comme notre champion! Qui veut essayer?
– Moi jé vé fais.
– [*to onlookers*] Voilà, nous avons déjà un amateur! Donc! mon frère si tu veux gagner 10 000 F [*to contestant*] i faut tu vas debout la chose-là avec ton dé bras ti as compris?
– Ja bien compris!
– Bon! faut fait!
– Wala-ça! Envoyé ton wari-là.

(quoted in Simard 1994: 26)

haltères (standard French): 'dumbbells'; *vé*: veux; *wari* (local Dioula language): 'money'.

■ Can you work out the meaning of the non-standard parts of this dialogue?

■ What features of pronunciation, grammar and vocabulary make them 'non-standard'?

■■ What seems to govern the switching between French and FPI?

A column signed 'Moussa' in the weekly newspaper *Ivoire-Dimanche*, written in a somewhat stylized version of FPI, became so celebrated that this language variety is sometimes referred to as *français de Moussa*. Here are one or two examples (from Lafage 1988):

Actièlement, les Toubalous i dit que c'é capote selment ça moyen bloqué sida
('*Pour l'instant, les Blancs disent que seuls les préservatifs protègent du sida*')

On dit que y a pas larzent dans péi mais les bagnes ça sort selment, c'é quel affair ça?

('*On dit qu'il n'y a pas d'argent dans ce pays mais les belles bagnoles ça fleurit. Qu'est-ce que ça veut dire hein?*')

Français façon la, y a pas son deux!
('*Rien n'égale ce drôle de français*')

▪▪ Some linguists consider *français populaire ivoirien* best regarded as a different (though related) language, rather than just a variety of French. Why?

(c) Much closer to 'international French' are examples like the following from Cameroon (from Tabi Manga 1990). Similar usages (sometimes identical ones) are found throughout francophone Africa:

Essomba ne paie pas le taxi, il voyage njoh

njoh: Douala word meaning 'free of charge'.

Les motaristes qui accompagnent le Président de la République sont vêtus de blanc

motariste: motorcyclist.

Déposez-moi à l'aviation

aviation: airport.

Ce n'est pas la peine d'entrer, le directeur a voyagé

voyager: to go away on a journey.

Meka a enceinté Edima

enceinter: to make pregnant.

And a recent collection of particularly picturesque items (Krop 1995) takes as its title the Ivory Coast phrase *faire l'avion par terre* ('être très pressé').

▪ Each of these examples illustrates a different type of lexical innovation (borrowing from another language, change of meaning, change in grammatical use of a standard French term, etc.) Can you specify the various types?

■■ How appropriate is the designation *français régional* in this case, as compared with the varieties in (a) and (b) above?

(d) Especially far removed from the sentences under (a) is the kind of French sometimes written or spoken by members of the educated African elite, who, when using French, often attach so much importance to avoiding colloquialisms and regionalisms that they risk sounding 'hypercorrect' or 'bookish'. Here is an excerpt from a letter to a colleague (by a Cameroon national) accompanying the return of a defective tape recorder:

A n'en pas douter votre surprise est grande de constater que je vous retourne votre magnétophone. Mais pour ne rien vous cacher, il n'a pas cessé de faire des siennes depuis le jour où vous me l'avez remis. En effet, outre les problèmes de lecture que vous me signaliez déjà lors de notre entrevue à Paris, il s'est posé un problème d'enregistrement avec, en prime, une destruction systématique des cassettes. Le sort subi par les deux cassettes que vous m'aviez remises ... m'a donc amené à faire mon deuil dudit magnétophone ... Sur ce, je mets un terme à ce petit pli en vous rappelant que je me tiens à votre disposition pour toutes informations supplémentaires.

(quoted in de Féral 1994: 44)

■ What features suggest that this is written by a highly competent 'second-language francophone'?

■■ What attitudes towards standard French and towards African varieties might account for these hypercorrections?

A full range of gradations along the 'language-interference scale' is seen the following Ivory Coast examples (Duponchel 1979: 408). All the sentences have the same (or virtually the same) meaning.

1   a ka mobili pousser
2   a ka mobili nyoni
3   faut pousser camion là
4   faut l'pousser c'te bagnole

5   il serait nécessaire de déplacer l'auto
6   il faut pousser l'auto
7   ke gi le kẽ ɛɛ
8   na ka pousser camion là

na ka: from 'il n'y a qu'à'.

■   Arrange them in order, from local African language (Alladian and Dioula both figure here) through to standard, perhaps even somewhat bureaucratic, French.

■■ At what point is comprehension likely to become possible for a speaker of a European or Canadian variety?

■■■ Select some of the forms and expressions mentioned in this chapter, and see how many of them are known to francophone friends and acquaintances (whether from metropolitan France or elsewhere). How seriously do they take them, and would they ever use them themselves? What conclusions does your enquiry enable you to reach about the international nature of French?

Further reading

Francard (1990) provides an excellent videocassette illustrating Belgian usages (with accompanying handbook). Dumas (1987) is an entertaining account of Quebec pronunciation intended for the non-specialist. Chapter 4 of Sanders (1993) covers grammatical and lexical features of Canadian French as well as phonetics. A wide range of European and non-European varieties are described in Valdman (1979). Several collections of non-metropolitan words and expressions (African in particular) have been published in recent years. See, for example, Depecker (1988) and Krop (1995).

•   •   •

French and Creole

Creoles and their origin

Early in the seventeenth century, French settlements were established on various Caribbean and Indian Ocean islands, as well as around the mouth of the Mississippi (modern Louisiana) and on the mainland of South America (French Guyana) (see Maps 7.1 and 7.2). Although the African colonies were not to come into being for another two centuries, a small number of trading posts, or *comptoirs*, were established along the West African coast.

By the end of the century a link between metropolitan France, the *comptoirs* and the islands was being provided by the slave trade. In the course of one triangular journey, a ship would transport three different kinds of cargo: 'colonial' produce (coffee, sugar, etc.), manufactured goods and slaves for the plantations.

■ Draw the triangle, showing where each type of cargo originated, its destination and the mode of payment.

Similar links, of course, existed between other maritime European states and their sub-tropical colonies; in some cases, conflicts between the European powers resulted in colonies being transferred from one to another.

■ Name and locate some specific French, British, Portuguese and Dutch 'plantation islands', including ones which have changed hands, and giving examples both from the Caribbean and the Indian Ocean. In each case indicate the date of first settlement and the date of any change of colonial power.

■ To which islands or groups of islands do the following French terms refer?

les Antilles; *les Mascareignes*; *l'île Maurice.*

It was the combined effects of the initial colonization and the subsequent slave trade that gave these territories their distinctive patterns of population, culture and language. The term *creole* is relevant to all three of these aspects.

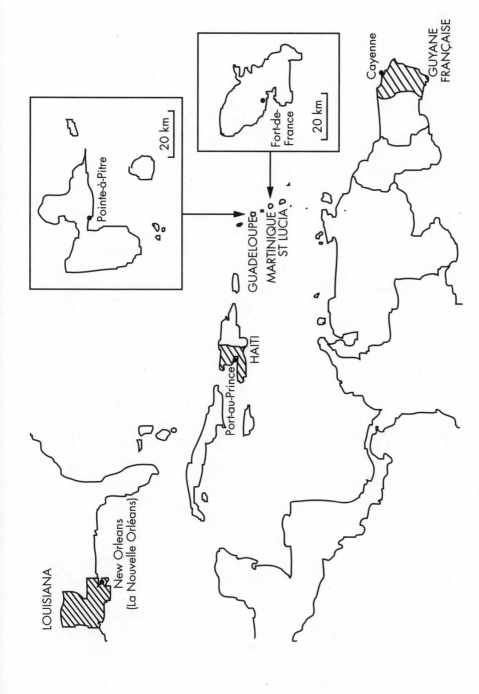

MAP 7.1   Principal French creole areas of the Caribbean

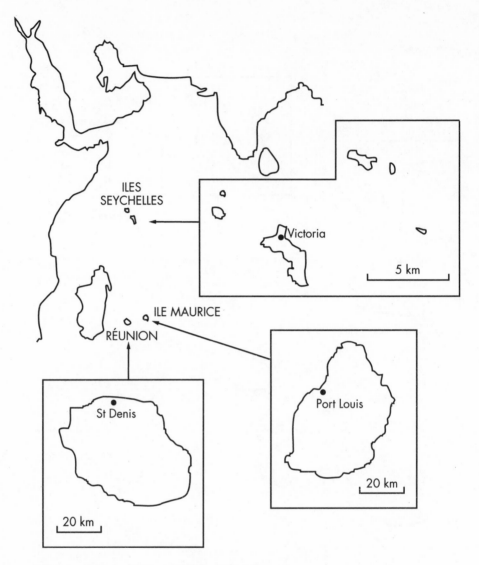

MAP 7.2   French creole areas of the Indian Ocean

When applied to populations, its exact meaning varies according to time and place, as the following definition indicates:

> ... aux Antilles comme aux Mascareignes, dans la première moitié du XVIIᵉ siècle, le qualificatif «créole» peut être appliqué aussi bien à des Blancs qu'à des Noirs. Cependant ... les significations du mot ont évolué de façon différente selon les lieux et les sociétés. Aux Antilles, le terme a été progressivement réservé à la désignation des Blancs nés

dans les îles tandis qu'en revanche, à l'île Maurice, «créole» ne peut qualifier que des Métis ou des Noirs (de phénotype africain) à l'exclusion des Blancs et des Indo-Mauriciens. Seul le créole réunionnais paraît avoir conservé le sens ancien puisqu'à la Réunion, «créole» désigne les Blancs, les Noirs ou les Métis nés dans l'île.

(Chaudenson 1979: 11)

■ What basic categories of population are to be found on the islands, judging from this description?

■■ How do you think each of them originated?

Clearly, despite all these variations, neither of the following categories of island dweller could be referred to as a 'creole':

– a slave newly arrived on the plantation (during the slavery period).
– a civil servant transferred from Paris (nowadays in one of the overseas departments).

■ Why not?

Créole is also applied to a wide range of 'cultural artefacts', for example in *riz (à la) créole*; *entremets à la créole*; *musique créole*; *coiffure à la créole*.

■ What do all these seem to have in common that justifies the use of the term?

But the most distinctive of all creole cultural artefacts are the creole languages themselves. Here is a recent translation into the Creole of the Seychelles Islands of a few lines from St Mark's Gospel. (The spelling used here is closely modelled on that of standard French – to obtain an impression of the actual pronunciation, see the phonetic transcription that follows.)

Chapite 3
Un zomme qui enna lamain desecher

Chapter 3

Jesus ti entrer encore dans leglise Juif, cote i ti voir un zomme ec un lamain desecher. Dimoune qui ti la ti veille Jesus pou voir si i ti a gueri

On another occasion when Jesus went to the synagogue, he saw a man there who had a withered hand. The people who were present watched

121

sa zomme jour sabbat, pour zote capabe accuse li. Jesus ti dire sa zomme ec lamain desecher, «Deboute la dans milieu!» Alors Jesus ti demande zote, «Esqui laloi Bondieu i permette nous faire dubien jour sabat, ousoit dumal; sauve lavie oubien touyer?» Tout dimoune ti rester tranquille.

Jesus to see whether he would cure him on the Sabbath, so that they could bring a charge against him. He said to the man with the withered hand, 'Come and stand out here.' Then he turned to them: 'Is it permitted to do good or to do evil on the Sabbath, to save life or to kill?' Everyone kept silent.

Phonetic transcription of the first sentence:

zezi ti ãtre ãkɔː dã legliz zwif, kote i ti vwa ɛ̃ zɔm ɛk ɛ̃ lamɛ̃ desese.

■ Can you translate the title? (For *enna*, think of *il y en a.*)

This is an example of what, for obvious reasons, is known as a French-based creole. (Other colonial situations gave rise to creoles based on English, Dutch, Portuguese and Spanish.) Particularly in the written form, though less so in phonetic transcription, there are several words in this passage which are identical or virtually identical in French and in Creole (e.g. *desecher*: French *dessécher*, 'dry out, desiccate').

■ Find some further examples.

Other words, though still having a strong resemblance to their French equivalents, have evidently undergone noteworthy changes, either in their appearance:

zomme; ec; i; pou; ousoit

or else in their meaning:

cote; Bondieu

or else in their appearance and their meaning:

dimoune.

■ Can you specify the French equivalents and work out what seems to have happened in these cases?

That leaves *ti* and *zote*, which probably don't bring anything obvious to mind, and *a*, which is not what it might seem. These will be explained shortly.

'Creole French', as illustrated here, is a product of the social conditions which existed on the islands during the slavery period. The use of African languages was forbidden on the plantations, and, in any case, in order to reduce the risk of mutiny or revolt, Africans from the same linguistic or ethnic groups were separated as far as possible, both during the voyage and after arrival. This made it essential for the slaves to acquire some French, as much in order to communicate with one another as with their masters. The present-day creoles appear to derive from the 'foreigners' French' of the first generation of slaves. This became the native language of the second and subsequent generations, and eventually also that of the white or mixed-race descendants of the slave-owners. The result today is that Creole is the mother tongue of all those born and brought up in the 'creolophone territories'.

Some structural features

The scarcity of direct evidence relating to the origin of creoles has led to a good deal of controversy over the extent to which their structure might have been influenced by the native speech of the slaves. Some linguists believe that the French creoles derive from *pidgins* – mixed Franco-African speech forms used in the earliest contact situations. Others see little or no evidence of African elements in material of the sort that has just been quoted, preferring to attribute the differences between French and the French-based creoles to the fact that early European settlers on the islands were uneducated provincials (mainly from north-western France, like the settlers in Quebec). They would have spoken dialects that were themselves already very far removed from the Paris standard – either of their own day or of ours – and *these* varieties were the point of departure for the modern creoles.

Certainly unfamiliar items such as *zote* and *ti* in the excerpt above turn out to be less strange when they are associated with regional or colloquial expressions like *eux autres* (*eux aut'*, [øzot]), or *étais* (as in *j'étais à entrer*). In the Creole of the Seychelles Islands, *zote* is in fact simply an equivalent of 'they'; the 'particle' *ti*, when placed before a verb like *entrer*, indicates the past tense, or, in the absence of a verb, serves as the past tense of 'to be'.

■ Locate examples of each of these three uses in the Seychelles Creole excerpt given above.

In this Creole, as in several others, *a* before a verb marks the future, and evidently derives from *(v)a* (cf. *il va manger*, etc.).

■ In the excerpt, *ti* combines with *a* in *ti a gueri*, which translates as 'would cure' (or 'was going to cure'). Why should this be the meaning?

The following further New Testament passage contains more examples of *zote*, as well as some other creole tenses, each of which again consists of one or two particles followed by a verb root. First read it through, comparing it with the translation.

Jesus ec son banne discipe ti alle aubord lamer Galilee, et un grand quantiter dimoune ti suive zote. Zote ti'ne sorti . . . dans canton lo lote coter lariviere Jourdain, et dans canton autour laville Tir ec Sidon. Sa grand lafoule ti vine cote Jesus acause zote ti'ne entende qui quantiter quec-chose i ti ape faire. Alors Jesus ti dire son banne discipe prepare un canote pou li, pengar sa lafoule ti a capabe crase li. I ti'ne gueri un grand quantiter dimoune, alors banne qui ti malade ti faire maniere pou touche li. Chaque fois qui banne mauvais lesprit ti voir li, zote ti tombe devant li, zote ti crier, «Ou Garson Bondieu!» Mais Jesus ti tout letemps reprimande zote pou zote pas faire dimoune conner qui i ti eter.

Jesus went to the lakeside with his disciples, and great numbers of people followed them. They had come from . . . Transjordan and the neighbourhood of Tyre and Sidon. This huge crowd came to Jesus because they had heard about all the things he was doing. So Jesus told his disciples to have a boat ready for him, to save him from being crushed by the crowd. For he had cured so many that sick people of all kinds came up to touch him. Each time the evil spirits saw him, they fell at his feet and cried, "You are the Son of God". But Jesus kept insisting that they should not make him known.

In passing, note how the following words have changed their meaning between French and Creole.

banne (from *bande*); *pengar* (from *prends garde*)

- Can you specify more precisely what has happened in these cases?
- Can you find other vocabulary features that call for comment?

The following tenses (in addition to the *ti* past) are illustrated in this excerpt: pluperfect (*li ti'ne gueri*: 'he had cured'); imperfect (*li ti ape faire*: 'he was doing').

The particle *'ne* is a contracted form of *fine* (hence the apostrophe); *li 'ne gueri* (= *li fine gueri*) means 'he has cured' and goes back to a regional French expression *il a fini de guérir*.

- Why does the combination of *ti* and *'ne* result in a pluperfect?

The particle *ape* by itself gives a 'progressive present' tense of a kind not found in standard French (*li ape gueri* = 'he is curing'). It relates to the *après* found in regional expressions like *il est après à guérir* (= standard 'il est en train de guérir').

- Why does the combination of *ti* and *ape* result in an imperfect?

Note that the 'simple present' tense 'he cures' would be *li gueri*.

The Creole of the Seychelles is basically similar to that spoken on Mauritius, which is illustrated in the following report from a local newspaper.

> Rajesh Soomaroo, chauffeur de taxi, et son cousin Deepak Soodoo, ont vécu un véritable cauchemar aux petites heures du matin, hier. Le véhicule de Rajesh venait de Trou d'Eau Douce quand le chauffeur a senti son véhicule flotter:
> «*Nous étions en train de rouler dans les parages de Bambous-Virieux. Il pleuvait à torrents. Ene coup, nou senti machine-là flotter*», explique-t-il. Il devait poursuivre en expliquant qu'il a tenté d'ouvrir la porte du véhicule, ainsi que les fenêtres, mais rien n'y faisait. Pendant ce temps, la voiture continuait toujours à dériver et ils

avaient franchi une distance de 300 mètres environ, tout en étant dans la voiture.

«*Seye ouvert la porte, ouvert la fenêtre, pas capav. Ceinture sécurité narien pas ti lé largué. Par la grâce Bon Dié, nou fine réissi largue ceinture, ouvert la fenêtre ek toit ouvrant. Lère guette déhors, nou trouve loto pé allé lor la rivière. Lère là nou compran ki fine arrivé. La rivière fine débordé, pé charrié nou*», a-t-il dit.

M. Soodoo a fait ressortir que leurs efforts pour ouvrir les portières de la voiture se sont avérés vains. «*Nou pas ti éna lotte choix ki sorti par la fenêtre. Lère nou jette lécorps, nou tombe dans dilo. D'après moi, ti éna dé bon mètre hauteur*», a-t-il estimé. Sur ce, il a expliqué que le courant les a emportés, mais qu'il ne pouvait dire pendant combien de temps ils devaient aller au gré des flots.

«*Pas capav dire combien létemps nou fine rester dan dilo. Mais séki mo capav dire, séki nou fine trouve la mort. Lère là, miracle fine arrivé. Alors ki courant ti pé charrié nou, nou fine gagne banne obstacles, banne débris. Pieds banane, l'herbe, feuillage fine bloque nou. Lère là, nou né pli casse la tête are loto, fini are li. Ti faire tellement noir ki pas même touve loto allé*», a-t-il fait ressortir.

(L'Express, 15 March 1995)

■■ With the help of the parts of the story that are in standard French, attempt a translation of the utterances in italics.

Here are some sentences in various other creoles. Caribbean creoles are not mutually comprehensible with the Indian Ocean varieties, but they nevertheless show many basic resemblances. The spelling conventions used in all these cases (including Mauritian this time) are much closer to actual pronunciation than in the earlier excerpts.

Guadeloupe	Anmizé-zot: 'Enjoy yourselves'
Louisiana	Mo sipozé vini bonè: 'I'm supposed to come early'
Guyana	Pandan Atipa té ka palé ye di ayen: 'While Atipa was talking, they said nothing'

ka is a particle of disputed origin found in many of the French Caribbean Creoles (according to one theory it may be related to *n'a qu'à*). Here it indicates the 'progressive aspect' (*-ing* form).

Martinique	Man pa ka bwè wonm: 'I don't drink rum'

ka in this case indicates the habitual present tense.

Guadeloupe   An pa konnèt se nonm-la ki vini la: 'I don't know the men who came'

Mauritius   Zo'n aret vin get nu: 'They've stopped coming to see us'

zo'n is a contraction of *zot fin*; *get* is related to French *guetter*.

■■ Explain why these sentences mean what they do, commenting on similarities and differences between the various creoles.

Particularly noteworthy are various pronunciation features shared by French-based Creoles of the Indian Ocean and the Caribbean alike, and showing the same differences from standard French. Table 7.1 shows the main correspondences between the latter and the Creoles.

TABLE 7.1

French	Creole
[ʃ] (as in *chat*)	[s]
[ʒ] (as in *jeu*)	[z]
[ø] (as in *peu*)	[e]
[y] (as in *sur*)	[i]
[ʀ] (as in *rat*)	[w] before a vowel (otherwise silent)

■ Find illustrative examples in:

– the IPA transcript of Seychelles Creole given earlier
– the excerpts you have been working through
– the following French/Martiniquais Creole equivalences:

Portugal: *Potigal*
Hongrie: *Ongwi*
Paris: *Pawi*
Russie: *Wisi*
l'Europe: *Lewop*

■■■ Though the creoles were long considered to be merely varieties of French, today it is usual to regard them as independent languages. What justification can you find for one or the other view?

Aspects of the sociology of the creoles

Data

- Fill in the gaps in Table 7.2.

■■ Related points: can you think of explanations?

- The local Creole has lower status in Guadeloupe and Martinique than in Haiti or the Seychelles.
- The Creole of Louisiana is of largely 'folkloric' value nowadays.
- The absence of any standard or regional French in St Lucia has actually tended to favour the position of the Creole.

■■■ It should be obvious even from the limited information given in Table 7.2 that there are major linguistic, social, political and economic differences between the 'creolophone' territories. Choose two or more contrasting places, and compare them under these four headings, using the more detailed accounts in the Bibliography as sources of further information.

Diglossia and multilingualism

The relationship between creoles and other languages in the 'creolophone' territories is typically a *diglossic* one (see p. 45). Some aspects of this are illustrated in the following excerpt from an interview with a working-class Martiniquais.

– Parlez-vous créole avec votre femme?
– Oui, presque toujours.
– Avec vos enfants?
– Le français mais quelquefois le patois.
– Avec vos amis . . . ?
– Le créole, tout le monde se connaît.
– Et avec votre employeur?
– Français, sauf quand il est en colère il parle créole, mais avec les autres employés je parle toujours en créole.
– Avec une personne que vous ne connaissez pas?
– Je parle toujours en français, mais on peut continuer en créole si l'autre est plus à l'aise dans le créole.

TABLE 7.2

	Zone Car(ibbean) or I(ndian) O(cean)	Population	GDP per capita (US $)	Political status	Former colonial power(s)	Official language(s)	Other languages (apart from Creole)	Proportion of Creole speakers in the indigenous population	Proportion of monolingual Creole speakers
								H(igh), L(ow), N(one)	
French Guyana	Car		2,000	DOM	F	Fr	—	H	L
Guadeloupe			6,000		F	Fr	—	H	L
Haiti		6.4m	400	Republic	F	Fr, Creole	—	H	H
Louisiana			21,100	State of USA	F → USA	Eng	Fr	L	N
Martinique			4,000					H	L
Mauritius	IO		1,950		F → GB			H	L
Réunion			5,000					H	L
Seychelles			4,170					H	L
St Lucia			1,810		F → GB	Eng	—	H	L

Note: Figures for the numbers of speakers of the various languages are often not available and are unreliable when they are, so the last two columns aim merely to give an approximation by means of the categories H, L and N.

– Et quand vous êtes en colère?

– Quand je suis fâché le français me dépasse, parce que peut-être je vais oublier quelque chose. Quand je ris, quand j'écoute des histoires c'est en créole; en français on ne rigole pas.

(Valdman 1978: 321–2)

■ What clues are given here about the relative status of French and Creole?

■■ The speaker refers to Creole as a *patois*. What does this reveal about his attitude to it?

■■ Why do you think he encourages his children to speak French?

This person is fortunate enough to be bilingual, as are most people these days in the départements d'outre-mer (DOM). But in Haiti, over 85 per cent of the population speak only Haitian Creole. The following account evokes the unenviable situation of the monolinguals.

The state functions like a perverted private enterprise by which the tiny elite – French-speaking, Catholic, predominantly foreign-educated and light-skinned – lives off the labour of the larger population, which remains predominantly peasant, Creole-speaking, illiterate, voodoo-practising and dark-skinned. By levying extortionate taxes on agricultural production, and by granting to a select few among the elite the monopolies to import necessities, those in power in the capital have drawn out the wealth that once had been shared among the peasants, until, during the last few decades, the exhausted land, deforested and eroded, began to consume itself.

(Danner 1993)

■ What economic factors make creole monolingualism so widespread in Haiti?

■■ Specify in as much detail as you can the nature of the Haitian 'language trap'.

The promotion, during the last few years, of Haitian Creole to the rank of national language and its gradual entry into the broadcast and written media suggests that its lowly status is beginning to change, though obviously there is a very long way to go yet. The restoration of democratic rule in 1995 may be a further encouraging factor.

Similar improvements in the status of creole have been occurring in other independent creolophone states and even in the DOM: it is now possible, for example, to take a degree in Creole Studies at the University of the Antilles. And everywhere there has been a striking increase in the output of serious novels, plays and poetry in Creole.

■■■ What are the chances of these societies one day becoming bilingual (or multilingual) rather than diglossic, and what, in practice, would such a transformation entail?

A classic example of linguistic diversity within a small population is to be found on Mauritius, where over a dozen languages are in use, including several Indian and Chinese dialects. Of the three main Mauritian languages, Creole is a universally spoken 'Low' language (see p. 45), French enjoys favour among the educated elite and is still the mother tongue of some islanders, while English is the language of government and administration. One result is trilingual newspaper reports like the following:

> Deux des trois accusés, à savoir Kressensing Hardowar et Mme Georgina Antoine, ont plaidé coupables d'importation de 60,77 g d'héroïne à Maurice. Hardowar est défendu par sir Gaëtan Duval QC, assisté de Mes Mario Hélène et Rama Valayden. Mme Antoine a retenu les services de Me Jean-Claude Bibi. Deux autres témoins ont déposé, en l'occurrence MM I. Mulloo, *Reservation Manager d'Air Mauritius* et l'inspecteur Jugdish Nundkishore.
>
> Le témoin Jean Clifford Bagniaux a maintenu avoir dit à un ami d'informer la police qu'il devait se rendre à Bombay, en compagnie des accusés, pour aller chercher du *Brown Sugar*. Il a précisé n'avoir pas participé à ce voyage, *parce ki ti pé fer travail bien sale ki ène danger pou la société*. Le témoin a ajouté *mo ti tire ène plan ki mo motocyclette en panne pou mo vine en retard pou mo pas alle dans l'Inde*.
>
> Présentant sa motion de *No case to answer*, Me Ollivry devait déclarer qu'il n'y a pas *evidence to show what took place in India. Where is the causing to import heroin?* s'est-il demandé. Lui donnant la réplique, Me Boolell a déclaré qu'il appartient à la Cour d'accepter le témoignage de Bagniaux ou de le rejeter. *There is enough evidence to show the participation of accused No 2, who is one of the chains to transport heroin in Mauritius*, devait-il soutenir.
>
> (*L'Express*, 15 March 1995)

■ What do the personal names tell us about the multicultural nature of the island?

■■ What is the function of each of the three languages here?

Symbolism and identity

Although they are French citizens, *Antillais* residing in metropolitan France experience serious identity problems:

> On les appelle les Neg'zagonaux. Ils n'aiment pas ça, mais reconnaissent que le terme est assez juste. «On a deux passeports: l'un français, l'autre de sale gueule.» Ils sont plus de 600 000 Antillais à vivre à Paris et en région parisienne, de quoi constituer un cinquième département d'outre-mer dans l'Hexagone. Pas une famille de Guadeloupe ou de Martinique qui n'ait un membre de sa famille en métropole . . . Chassés des îles par un chômage qui touche 30% de la population, beaucoup de jeunes trouvent en métropole un emploi aux PTT ou dans les hôpitaux. Un salaire et beaucoup de solitude . . . Parce qu'ici, on n'est jamais que français «à part». Sentiment d'altérité renforcé par le voyage annuel aux Antilles pour lequel beaucoup de familles antillaises se sacrifient tout le reste de l'année, et le projet de retourner un jour «au pays». 5% d'entre eux seulement réalisent ce rêve.
>
> (*Libération*, 26 February 1991)

■ Can you explain the term *Neg'zagonal*?

■ What is meant by the reference to the 'two passports'?

Here are some accounts of situations in which symbolic importance attaches to the use (or non-use) of Creole by expatriates from the DOM/TOM.

1 Albert is a post-office sorter in metropolitan France.

> Dans la cour, les gars n'ont jamais fini. Les sacs ne cessent pas d'arriver. Ils sont tous antillais les gars. Sauf les pointeurs, bien entendu. Les pointeurs, c'est ceux qui surveillent les opérations. Les petits chefs, quoi. Ils sont tous métros, les pointeurs.

Moi, je suis antillais. La Guadeloupe, vous connaissez? C'est beau la Guadeloupe.

Mi péyi-la – An plin mitan lanmé – I la – Kon bato – Mi Dézirad la – Mi Lèsint la – Dominik anba.

Après, il y a eu une altercation sur le bitume, entre Albert qui était en train de discuter avec Benjamin Urbain, et un pointeur. C'est toujours pareil. Si on voit un Noir en train de discuter, on lui tombe dessus. Si c'est un Européen, il peut parler toute la journée. Alors Albert et Benjamin se sont fait engueuler.

– Écrasez-vous un peu avec votre patois p'tit nègre!

C'est le langage de nos parents. Ça fait mal. Alors Albert s'est rebiffé et a laissé éclater sa rancoeur et a engueulé celui qui l'engueulait, et ils se sont bien engueulés. Et puis ça s'est terminé comme d'habitude.

– Si ça ne te plaît pas mon vieux, tu n'as qu'à rentrer chez toi!

(Lemoine 1982: 296)

2   Marcelle, also from Guadeloupe, works at a reception counter in a Paris social security office.

– Monsieur, demande Marcelle . . . vous désirez?

Il se penche en avant, la fixe un instant, lève les sourcils comme s'il venait de découvrir quelque chose, sourit, oublie le portefeuille qu'il cherchait.

– *Ou ka palé créyol?*

Marcelle se raidit, blessée jusqu'au fond des fibres. Derrière, elle discerne le souffle des filles qui écoutent, intéressées, les filles qui n'en perdent pas une bouchée. Son regard se fait dur, tranche comme une lame d'acier.

– Je regrette, je ne comprends pas.

– *Ou pa ka palé créyol?*

Le type fronce les sourcils. Marcelle n'aime pas du tout le genre qu'il a pris. Elle le lui fait bien sentir. Imagine-t-il qu'elle n'est pas capable de s'exprimer en français? Et les collègues qui ricanent . . . Dans le service, on l'accuse déjà de faire du racisme anti-Blanc, et lui arrive tout content, *ou pa ka palé créyol*, cet imbécile . . .

– Mais de quel pays êtes-vous, reprend l'Antillais qui s'entête, qui la dévisage avec effronterie. Parce que moi je suis de la Guadeloupe et je croyais . . .

– Je connais également la Guadeloupe, mais vous savez, je parle très bien le français.

(Lemoine 1982: 287)

3   Benjamin has just arrived in Paris from Martinique and needs to ask for street directions.

Chance. Une silhouette familière débouche de l'intersection la plus proche. Une démarche tranquille et un air dégagé. Un Noir. Comme lui, en quelque sorte. Un Antillais. Il le laisse s'approcher, lui sourit, l'arrête d'un geste de la main.
– *Côté la rue dé Pwasionié, yé*?
Le grand type le regarde, ouvre de grands yeux interloqués.
– Alors là mon vieux hein, si tu veux qu'on te comprenne, il va falloir apprendre le français!
– *Ou pa ka palé créyol*, jette Benjamin stupéfait et déconcerté.
– Qu'est-ce que tu racontes, mon vieux, essaie de t'expliquer comme un civilisé, on n'est plus chez les sauvages, ici!
– Tu ne parles pas créole, reprend Benjamin décontenancé et piqué au vif, en prenant soin cette fois de s'exprimer en français, mais d'où sors-tu? Où donc es-tu né?
– Alors là mon vieux hein, moi je suis né au Mali, hein, à Bamako. D'où tu débarques, toi?
– Moi, des Antilles. Je suis français, mais des Antilles. Je suis Antillais.
L'autre le regarde . . . éclate soudain d'un rire énorme venu du fond mystérieux des forces de l'Afrique, un rire qui . . . monte jusqu'aux nuages, retombe, démesuré, aux pieds du petit Antillais, qui le regarde, qui ne sait plus où il en est, le petit Antillais qui se prend pour un Français.

(Lemoine 1982: 59)

■■ In each case, outline and account for the attitude of the various participants towards Creole.

■■ What is the relationship between a person's attitude towards Creole and their sense of identity?

■■ In what way does the third episode illustrate the notion *français à part* used in the earlier excerpt from *Libération* (p. 132)?

■■■ Find out about some of the linguistic and sociological features of English-based creoles, and draw as many parallels as you can with the French-based ones.

■■■ What would be the advantages and disadvantages of a state having a creole as official or co-official language?

Further reading

On creoles in general, see Todd (1990) for an introduction and the articles collected in Arends *et al.* (1995) for more detail. See also Fasold (1990). Chaudenson (1995) deals more specifically with French-based creoles; these are also the subject of Chapter 11 of Sanders (1993). An interesting description of the linguistic complexities of the island of Mauritius is to be found in Baker (1972). *Quid* is a useful source of basic facts and figures for the various places referred to in this chapter.

•   •   •

Chapter 8

The use of French
by immigrants

Immigration in francophone Europe

The picture of variation that has emerged so far will be incomplete unless account is taken of the use made of French by the immigrants who have settled – temporarily or permanently – in the developed francophone countries.

In the nineteenth century, much of the 'immigrant' workforce in Paris and other urban centres came from rural (often non-French-speaking) areas of the Hexagon itself or from neighbouring parts of Belgium. But the later nineteenth century and the first few decades of the twentieth saw an influx from southern and eastern Europe into France, and also into Wallonia and Switzerland.

In the economic boom years of the 1950s and 1960s, there was a new wave of immigration, this time predominantly from North Africa and the Iberian peninsula. In Belgium and Switzerland during the same period there was much immigration from former Yugoslavia and Turkey. Assimilation is still in many respects incomplete and the most recent immigrants tend to occupy the lowliest social positions and to perform the most menial functions – as did Italian or Polish immigrants earlier this century. Things are beginning to change with the 'second generation' (born in Europe), and language use, in particular, is an area where striking contrasts exist between this group and their parents.

Attitudes lag behind, though. The UN defines an 'immigrant' as a foreign national who has been authorized to reside in a given country for more than a year. But in practice, as P. Bernard has pointed out (Bernard 1993: 41), foreign bankers or diplomats who fit this definition are rarely considered as 'immigrants'. On the other hand, the children of 'migrant workers' are frequently so regarded, even if born in Europe and passport holders of a European state.

- What factors account for the differences between the official and the unofficial view of what constitutes an 'immigrant'?

As far as France is concerned, specific figures for immigration emerge as follows from census statistics and OECD surveys (after Bernard 1993).

In 1990, there were approximately 3.6 million resident foreign nationals. (Of these, rather less than 0.5 million were 'white collar immigrants', mainly from northern Europe and North America.) The principal places of origin (numbers to the nearest thousand) were:

Portugal	646,000
Algeria	620,000
Morocco	585,000
Italy	254,000
Spain	216,000
Tunisia	208,000
Turkey	202,000
Sub-Saharan Africa	172,000

Of all foreign nationals, 60 per cent were resident in just three French regions: Rhône-Alpes, Provence-Côte-d'Azur and, above all, Ile-de-France.

■■ What economic and other factors might account for this concentration?

To these 'first-generation' immigrants can be added the second and third generations: people who are of immigrant descent, but were themselves born in France and therefore have French nationality. An estimated 10 million people fall into this category, if we trace origins back to the beginning of the century. This means that one-fifth of French nationals have one or more non-French ancestors in the last three generations of their family. This includes such well-known figures as Pierre Bérégovoy (a former Premier), Nicolas Sarkozi (a former cabinet minister), François Cavanna (a writer and columnist), who are of Russian, Hungarian and Italian origin respectively. Cavanna has written an interesting autobiographical account of an Italian community in the Paris suburbs during the inter-war period (Cavanna 1978).

The first generation

Having for the most part arrived in Europe as adults, immigrants of this generation are far from being native francophones. Some features of their use of French are illustrated in the following conversational transcriptions.

(a)   (Speaker from Algeria)

Je suis vraiment – de toutes manières – moi je veux arriver à quelque chose. Depuis que j'ai rentré ici – j'peux pas sortirer comme ça. Comment? J'aime mieux faire mes huit heures comme ça – moi – carrément – carrément. Histoire d'arriver. C'est pas la question de la paie. La paie au chômage – c'est ce qu'il y a de plus. C'est pas une raison qu'il y a le paie le plus. C'est pas – Il est pas venu pour la paie là – il est venu pour pouvoir prendre à lire et écrire – mais maintenant – on n'arrive même pas dans la rue – on sait même pas ousqu'on y va quand même – hé.

(Heredia 1983: 100)

■   Can you identify items that would not be used by a native speaker of French?

■   How about items which would be, but which are colloquial?

■■ Why is the French of immigrant speakers so often full of examples of *français familier* or *populaire*?

(b)   (Interview with a Spanish speaker)

– Vous l'aviez connue avant de venir en France?
– Ah non! mais non, c'est porque yo habia metté une annonce sur un, journal *Figaro*, y elle me va escrir. Et ma une otra petite qui travaille à Paris me va mener.
– Vous aviez eu l'idée de mettre une annonce dans un journal?
– Ah oui! J'sabia pas, je voulais à travailler mais je ne connaissais pas personne. Et je vais à demander une fille qui travaillait à Paris qu'elle mette une annonce sur le journal. Me va mett' une annonce et après me van a escrir beaucoup de gens, comme ça de lettres . . . Mais yo min' idée era de ir à travailler à Paris. Et je vais aller à ver une dame, et juste en el moment de arriver, elle va faire une autre. Et après je vais aller à la dame à la côté de l'Arco de Triom' tout suite elle me va dire que oui.

(Heredia 1983: 101)

■   Once again, identify unidiomatic, ungrammatical and colloquial items.

■■ Why should speakers of Spanish be more prone than speakers of Arabic to 'language interference' like *sabia* for *savais*?

■■ What differences might you expect between this and the French of a Spanish student on a university language course?

Here are some mispronunciations commonly heard from first-generation hispanophone immigrants:

[de] (*des*) for *deux*;
[matʃin] (*matchine*) for *machine*
[abril] for *avril*
[menusie] (*ménoussier*) for *menuisier*
[ru] (*roue*) for *rue*
[parske] (*parce qué*) for *parce que*
[jur] (*your*) for *jour*

■■ If you know Spanish, can you explain the deviations of these speakers in terms of the sound system of their native language?

The excerpts quoted above, though not untypical, are just two from a range of possible examples. The degree of *code-switching* – i.e. extent to which speakers alternate between their first and second languages in the way seen in excerpt (b) – varies greatly from one individual to another, and so of course does their overall proficiency in French. Some of the determining factors emerge from the following portrait of a type of immigrant likely to make well-below-average progress in second-language acquisition.

> ...une femme, assez âgée, arrivée tard en France, ne travaillant pas hors de chez elle, s'occupant surtout de la maison, n'ayant de relations qu'avec les membres de sa famille et quelques voisins de même origine. Elle vivrait en périphérie urbaine, là où l'isolement et l'anonymat sont les plus grands, mais viendrait de la campagne. Enfin, elle serait monolingue, de langue maternelle non romane, et analphabète. Certaines immigrées maghrébines correspondent encore à cette description.
>
> (Heredia 1983: 115)

■ Judging from this extreme case, what environmental and personal circumstances would *favour* the acquisition of French by first-generation immigrants?

Attitudes and ambitions are also crucial in increasing or inhibiting motivation for language learning. Some immigrants feel they are merely temporary exiles and aim to return home one day. Others see themselves as permanent settlers, and may plan to become European citizens by naturalization. There is wide variation in the extent to which periodic short visits are made to the home country (in general, immigrants from the Iberian peninsula go back more often those from North Africa). And loss of cultural or religious identity through assimilation may or may not be a cause of concern: in an attempt to maintain their 'difference' some immigrants prefer to use French as little as possible, or deliberately conserve a strong accent.

■■ Making an appropriate selection from the various attitudinal and environmental factors mentioned so far, and adding any others that occur to you, produce your own portrait of:

   – an immigrant who makes average progress in acquiring proficiency in French
   – an immigrant whose progress is above average.

For many first-generation immigrants, whatever their level of fluency, the use of French tends to be restricted to the relatively impersonal 'informational' functions characteristic of the workplace, the social security office, the shopping centre, the public transport system, etc. The 'expressive' function so important in social life – within the family, for instance – is carried out by the native language. C. de Heredia expresses the consequences as follows:

> Le français, amputé de ses autres fonctions fondamentales . . . devient utilitaire, extérieur au locuteur qui répond à une communication au sens très restreint, minimale et obligée, et non à la communication réelle avec toutes ses composantes.
>
> (Heredia 1983: 121)

■■ Comment on this statement, giving some concrete examples of 'communication components' which might be lacking in the language use of many first-generation immigrants (e.g. expressing feelings, telling jokes, etc.).

The second generation

The children of the immigrants just discussed either arrived in Europe when very young or else were actually born in Europe. Consequently their linguistic background and competence are strikingly different from those of their parents. A case in point is 18-year-old Yamama, from a Moroccan family, interviewed in the early 1990s by Camille Lacoste-Dujardin. Having spent all her life in Nantes, Yamama's competence in French is indistinguishable from that of someone with purely French ancestry. Arabic is another matter, though:

> J'ai toujours parlé l'arabe avec mes parents, bon, l'arabe mélangé avec le français, quoi! Mais c'est quand même de l'arabe. Mais c'est vrai que lorsqu'on veut avoir une conversation qui sorte du commun, bon, on a des problèmes, parce qu'il y a des tas de mots qu'on ne connaît pas. Alors, on essaie de leur faire comprendre avec des petits mots, ou en français.
>
> (Lacoste-Dujardin 1992: 232)

Similar experiences are related by her Franco-Algerian friend, Fadela:

> Bon, côté discussion simple, je peux très bien discuter avec n'importe qui en arabe, ça va ... Maintenant, c'est devenu ... J'ai remarqué que j'ai plus de problèmes pour parler l'arabe dans certaines matières.
>
> (Lacoste-Dujardin 1992: 231)

- ■ What do you think Yamama means by 'petits mots' and Fadela by 'discussion simple'?

- ■■ What kinds of conversation do you think are beyond the scope of their Arabic?

- ■■ What factors enabled Yamama and Fadela to become so proficient in French, even though Arabic was the language used at home?

The less than perfect Arabic-language competence of such second-generation immigrants could be said to be the mirror image of the deficient French-language competence of their parents' generation. Table 8.1 shows the basic pattern (various other immigrant languages could be substituted for Arabic, depending on the individual concerned):

TABLE 8.1

	French (Generation 1)	Arabic (Generation 2)
Public use	+	−
Private use	−	+

■ How would you represent in diagrammatic form the Arabic of Generation 1 and the French of Generation 2?

■■ Contrast the two kinds of deficiency in more detail, bearing in mind that the first generation are in the process of *acquiring* French, and that the second generation are in the process of *losing* the 'ancestral language'. What kinds of use are the first to be acquired, and which are the last to be abandoned, and why?

Naturally, wide variation exists among individuals here as well, not only in their language competence, but also in their attitudes towards French on the one hand and their ancestral language on the other. To illustrate this, here are some further excerpts from C. Lacoste-Dujardin's interviews with second-generation immigrants in Nantes, together with some of her comments (Lacoste-Dujardin 1992: 229–32):

(a) La seule à déclarer ignorer totalement l'arabe marocain de ses parents est Houriya – réalité ou défi? Cinquième de [neuf enfants], elle a vécu entre un père rapidement discrédité, une mère active hors du foyer, bientôt émancipée, mais à qui Houriya fait grief de l'avoir confiée aux soins d'une grand-mère maternelle venue trouver refuge en France après maints déboires matrimoniaux (. . . sans pour autant l'entretenir dans l'usage de la langue). Ce n'est qu'aujourd'hui, à vingt-six ans, qu'Houriya espère se mettre à l'apprentissage de l'arabe, encouragée par le projet d'aller vivre au Maroc, avec son compagnon marocain, arrivé bébé en France comme elle.

(b) Elevée en Kabylie jusqu'à six ans, de parents berbérophones, Yasmina déclare ne pas parler . . . le kabyle, avec lequel elle a rompu en même temps qu'avec ses parents. Mais après six années de vie indépendante, elle a entrepris de suivre à Paris des cours de kabyle, au nom d'une curiosité qu'elle dit surtout intellectuelle, quoique non dénuée d'affectivité, peut-être prélude à une réconciliation qu'elle n'exclut plus avec ses parents?

berbérophone, kabyle: see p. 53.

(c)   Amina a fugué d'un foyer bientôt désuni. «A la maison, on ne parlait jamais . . . Je ne peux même plus dire aujourd'hui s'ils me parlaient en arabe ou en français; des fois tu ne reconnais pas. Mais on répondait en français. Moi, je ne peux pas parler l'arabe . . . Je comprends, mais je ne le parle pas . . . Non!» Amina, animatrice, considère son activité incompatible avec l'étude de l'arabe. «Après le bac, j'ai voulu l'apprendre un peu. Mais je travaillais en même temps et le boulot m'attirait plus que les études.»

(d)   . . . Ourdia et Faroudja ne se contentent pas de comprendre mais parlent aussi leur langue maternelle avec leurs parents, l'arabe, en l'occurrence. Faroudja se sent tout à fait bilingue: «J'allais à l'école, je parlais le français; je rentrais chez moi, à midi, c'était automatique, je parlais arabe.» Et aussi: «Avec mes copines et mes copains, je parle arabe facilement.»

(e)   *Yamama*: «Avec mes frères et ma soeur, on a plus tendance à parler, entre nous, en français, parce que c'est plus facile, ça passe plus vite. Avec mes parents, c'est toujours: «Ouais, vous êtes marocains. Parlez arabe! Quand vous allez retourner, qu'est-ce qu'ils vont dire de vous, là-bas?'»

■   Situate these various informants on a scale ranging from mono-lingualism to bilingualism, taking account of the difference between 'passive' and 'active' language knowledge (i.e. ability to understand and ability to speak).

The importance of non-linguistic factors emerges clearly from such testimonies. Inter-family and peer-group relationships, the degree of inte-gration in European society, the extent to which contacts are maintained with the 'home country': all these have a role to play.

■■   In each case, specify how such factors seem to affect language use and attitudes.

As is implied in excerpt (e), inadequate knowledge of the ancestral language can sometimes have disturbing consequences. Consider the following observation made by an adolescent about family visits to North Africa:

> ... si on passe ses vacances où il y a de la famille, il vaut mieux parler
> l'arabe ... Si j'arrive devant eux [et] leur parle en français, ils vont
> dire, qu'est-ce que c'est celui-là, c'est un étranger, tout ça, euh, alors
> je pense que c'est vraiment important.

The investigators comment:

> Cependant, [ces jeunes] affirment leurs difficultés à parler l'arabe
> dans ce contexte car ils sont souvent objet de risée et leur façon de
> manier l'arabe les désigne inévitablement comme immigré et les
> renvoie à leur incomplétude: «J'ose pas trop parler arabe». «Je
> parlais l'algérien comme un âne ..., comme un immigré».
>
> (Dabène and Billiez 1987: 68–9)

Indeed, statements like 'Ma langue est l'arabe, mais je ne la parle pas' are
quite often to be heard from second-generation *Maghrébins*.

■■ Why is such a statement only apparently a paradox, and what
   identity problems does it point to?

Alienation from the ancestral culture can go hand in hand with a sense of
not belonging fully to European society, either. Language may be a factor
here too: for instance, some *beurs* feel they need to change their name if
they are to have a chance of full integration, especially if they are French
nationals. (Some, but not all: many actually prefer to assert their cultural
difference.) Examples of surname changes are: Benbouali to Thiroux;
Azzouzi to Gastineau; Hamadi to Lemonier (*Le Nouvel Observateur*, 7
December 1995).

■■ What advantages and disadvantages can you see in a change of
   name? Consider the likely reactions of employers, family and peer
   group.

Such identity problems, and the range of individual variation in language
use and competence that has just been presented, are much more characteristic of young people with North African origins than they are of those
whose families come from Spain or Portugal. In the latter case, language
use follows a fairly straightforward and consistent pattern (Dabène and
Billiez 1987: 68): Portuguese or Spanish are used with parents or older
relatives; communication between brothers and sisters is typically in

French, and French is used for all 'external' or 'public' communication, as well as for interactions with the peer group. The same investigators point out that Maghreban immigrants – unlike Iberians – sometimes have recourse to the ancestral language even in peer-group conversations, as the following testimony shows:

> Avec les copains algériens, si on a plutôt quelque chose à cacher on parle en arabe . . . quand il y a du monde et qu'on veut parler devant eux, dans le car, et puis ça énerve les gens qu'on parle arabe, je sens que ça les énerve, alors on aime bien.
>
> (Dabène and Billiez 1987: 69)

Many possible reasons for these Iberian/North African differences come to mind. Factors may be political (the Maghreb countries are former French colonies), cultural (Islam vs Catholicism), geographical (the Iberian peninsula is more easily accessible for short visits than North Africa), ethnic (European vs non-European) or linguistic (French, Spanish and Portuguese are all Romance languages).

■■   Assess the likely importance of these various factors, and any others that may occur to you. Suggest how in practice their influence might operate.

Code-switching

Note should be taken of one further contrast between first- and second-generation speakers (whether Iberian or Maghreban). This involves 'code-switching' – the alternation between one language and another in the course of a conversation. The kind of code-switching illustrated by the first-generation Spanish speaker on p. 140 can plausibly be attributed to her inadequate command of French: she uses Spanish to fill in the gaps, as it were. By contrast, when practised by bilingual second-generation speakers, code-switching, instead of simply resulting from incompetence, allows various deliberate effects to be achieved.

The following examples are adapted from a study by Louise Dabène (1990: 164–7). According to her analysis, code-switching may, among other things:

(a)   highlight a personal comment:

(*To parent*): Yo mañana empiezo . . . me levanto a las siete de la mañana [*I start tomorrow . . . I get up at seven*]. J'suis malade rien de le savoir.

(b)   make it clear who is being spoken to when there is a change of addressee:

FATHER: Cuando tiene que levantarse . . . [*when she has to get up*]
DAUGHTER (*to father*):   ¡Oye! Me he levantado . . . [*Hey! I am up*]
(*to group*): La première fois que j'ai commencé au Quick – pendant une semaine: six heures du matin!

(c)   serve to introduce a more 'technical' statement:

(*To parent*):   ¿Cómo se abre esto? [*how do you open this?*] J'ai appuyé sur eject mais ça ne s'est pas ouvert.

(d)   permit slightly disrespectful imitations of 'elders and betters':

– Comment elle s'appelle ta fille?
– Andrea.
– (*imitating grandmother*) ¡Va buscar el pan, Andrea! [*go and get the bread, Andrea!*]

■   In each of these cases, say specifically how the effect is produced.

■■   Which code-switching effect is involved in the following, and how does it work?

– Je fais un BEP de plombier, moi.
– BEP de plombier?
– Ouais.
– C'est vrai?
– Ouais! C'est bien, comme ça je fais ma comptabilité tout seul.

– Après tu vas au Dzazair [*in Algeria*].

– Ih [*Yes*]. Nahdam [*I'm working*].

– tahdam [*You're working*].

– Euh, lalla [*Yes, Ma'am*].

– Ouh! šhai ʕandak swarad [*have you any money*]?

– Eh oui!

– ʕandak mra [*Have you a wife*]?

– Eh ben, non.

BEP: Brevet d'études professionnelles.

The influence of immigrants on language use

The linguistic versatility of second-generation immigrants has begun to have its effects on the speech of many young white francophones, particularly in the high-rise working-class suburbs of Paris and other urban centres. The proficiency of young *beurs* and *blacks* in using the ancient French tradition of back slang or *verlan* is discussed in Chapter 10. But some of their contributions to the language are more original and derive more specifically from their bilingual and bicultural background.

One notable feature is an influx of colloquial items derived from Arabic. Examples include: *zaama*! (a disapproving exclamation aimed at someone who is putting on airs); *ballak*! ('watch out!'); *avoir l'aïn* ('to have the evil eye, or bad luck'); *gône* ('kid' in the sense of 'teenager'); *chouffe*! '('look!') and *bellecq* ('perhaps').

■■ These novelties are to be distinguished from older, 'colonial' borrowings from Arabic which have been established for many years: *toubib* ('doctor'); *klebs* ('dog'); *baraka* ('good luck'). How do you think these found their way into French?

Also noteworthy is the trading of ritual insults known as *vannes* or *charres*. These relate to alleged (but wildly exaggerated and often highly obscene) characteristics of the interlocutor's family, and particularly the mother. The classic example, brought to a wider public by the satirical television programme *Les Guignols*, is *Ta mère, elle chausse du deux* ('Your mother takes size 20 shoes'). The origins here seem to be *black* as much as *beur*: this kind of language play has long been prevalent in the ghettos of North American cities. In France at least, such insults have considerable curiosity value outside the ghetto: published collections have recently begun to enter the best-seller market. However, their crucial role in 'inner-city' teenage culture is undiminished. Elaborate rules and conventions govern the verbal jousting and much prestige attaches to the winners. In particular, insults directed at the 'adversary's' mother seek to undermine the honour of the family as a whole.

■ Explain the following uses of «*ta mère*»:

Ta mère est tellement pauvre que c'est les éboueurs qui lui donnent les étrennes.

Ta mère a tellement de varices qu'elle n'a pas besoin de cartes routières.

Finally, rap, a distinctively black American tradition which has been readily and successfully adapted to a francophone environment. Its practitioners have been described as follows:

Enfants de l'immigration et de la galère, ils débarquent d'une autre France, celle des cités ghettos et des couloirs de métro. Avec leur fascination de l'Amérique et leur nostalgie de l'Afrique. Avec leurs looks insensés, moitié Rambo, moitié basketteur de Harlem. Avec leur langue, le verlan; leur musique, le rap.

(*Le Nouvel Observateur*, 9 August 1990)

■■ What cultural and social origins and influences are evoked here?

Here is a characteristic excerpt:

Un beau jour que j'avais sur moi plein de shit
Je me suis fait serrer par les schmits
J'ai agonisé sous les vapeurs du stick
Ils m'ont savaté pour me voler mon fric.

schmits: policiers; *stick*: joint.

■■ How do the three aspects of language use just considered reflect the ideology of the more rebellious and marginal *enfants des cités*: anti-bourgeois, anti-adult, fiercely proud of their ethnic group?

■■■ Is it an advantage or a disadvantage for young second-generation immigrants to be bilingual and bicultural?

■■■ What are the prospects for the maintenance of their ancestral languages by future generations of immigrants?

Further reading

Apart from the various items referred to in the text, relatively little seems to have been published on the topic treated in this chapter. However, in Chapter 5 of Sanders (1993), L.-J. Calvet describes the range of languages spoken by different immigrant groups in Paris, and their interrelationships.

•   •   •

Situational and social variation

The material for illustration in this chapter is based on the language varieties found in Paris and other urban centres in northern France. However, provided due allowance is made for certain regional features like those referred to in Chapters 5 and 6, similar general patterns are found elsewhere in francophone Europe and North America.

Levels of language

First, read the following:

> Je suis revenu à une heure et demie de Bougainville . . . je vois un mec affalé dans la rue, la vache, la gueule en sang . . . Puis d'un coup j'ai, j'ai vu deux trois bagnoles que, qui m'ont croisé, y a une certaine . . . bon bah, y'en a deux ou trois que, qu'ont dit, bon bah, moi j'peux rien moi, démerde-toi ça veut dire . . . et puis j'ai eu l'énorme chance de voir Max Brétavoine, un bon pote à moi j'lui dis P'tit Max téléphone à un, un docteur parce que . . . i' faut que . . . moi j'peux pas laisser l' . . . le lascar comme ça . . . j'suis resté une demi-heure avec le mec sur la . . . puis le mec j'osais pas l'bouger, la mobylette était complètement . . . elle était tombée dans un, dans un trou de poule, comme on dit, le mec tu vois . . . ce que je . . . bien ébréché, et puis y a un docteur qu'est venu puis P'tit Max Brétavoine, il a fait le boulot, il a été chercher un docteur par téléphone, le téléphone, il a été prévenu le docteur, il a été prévenu le mec, il est arrivé une demi-heure après.
>
> (quoted in Hauchecorne 1996)

- Can you outline the main events being recounted here?

- Which of the following is correct?

    - This is part of the evidence given by a policeman to the assembled judges and jurors in a court of law.
    - It is a workman describing a recent incident to family and friends over Sunday lunch.

–   It was recorded from a lecture about road safety delivered to her pupils by the headmistress of a *collège*.

–   It comes from the prize-winning autobiography of a distinguished local politician.

–   It is an excerpt from a typed and signed statement by a witness to a traffic accident.

■   What features of grammar, vocabulary, and general organization allow you to decide which is the most likely scenario, and which other scenarios to eliminate?

It should be clear from this exercise that linguistic features are linked to a variety of other factors, such as the age and sex of the speaker, the formality of the situation, the hierarchical relationships between the speakers (equals, inferiors or superiors), their social class, the nature of the medium (writing or conversation).

■■   In the light of this, can you explain the phrase 'socio-situational variation'?

Naturally it would be useful to be able to give a precise classification of items of vocabulary and grammar in terms of their non-linguistic implications. A number of different classifications have been proposed, though all have their drawbacks (see Sanders 1993 for discussion). There does at least seem to be general agreement that three basic levels or types of language are involved. These might be labelled *colloquial* (or *informal*), *neutral* and *formal* (Batchelor and Offord 1982 give a wide range of specific French examples).

Some variations in terminology should be noted at this point. Some writers (e.g. Batchelor and Offord 1982) refer to these formality levels as *registers*: others (e.g. Holmes 1992 or Wardhaugh 1992) speak of different *styles*, reserving the term *register* for the specialized forms of language used by particular occupational groups. Here the expression *levels of language* is used, and we concentrate on the way these levels correlate with the situations in which speakers find themselves. (The term *style* we apply to the administrative and other varieties of language discussed in Chapter 10.)

■■■   Follow up the references given here and in the 'Further reading' section, and attempt to give your own account of the way in which different commentators use the terms *register* and *style*.

Here are a few vocabulary items from the above excerpt, together with some synonyms:

mec; *lascar*; *homme*; *monsieur*; *type*;
gueule; *bouche*; *orifice buccal*;
la vache!; *mon Dieu!*; *juste ciel!*;
bagnole; *voiture*; *automobile*.

■   Assign each word or expression to one or other of the formality levels.

In francophone countries the 'colloquial' range is commonly subdivided into *français familier* and *français populaire*, the latter comprising those items which are judged to be typical of working-class usage. (The term *français vulgaire* is applied to utterances containing obscene or blasphemous items.) Corresponding to the middle, 'neutral' level is *français courant*, while *français cultivé* refers to the formal level (alternatives to the latter term are *français soigné*, *français soutenu* or *français littéraire*). Together, *français courant* and *français cultivé* constitute *le bon usage*, the norm presented in grammars, manuals for foreign learners, etc.

■   Allocate each of the utterances below to one (or more) of the following categories:

bon usage; *français cultivé*; *français courant*; *français familier*; *français vulgaire*.

Moi j'ai paumé vachement comme pognon quand ils m'ont viré hein.
J'ai perdu beaucoup d'argent quand ils m'ont licencié.
J'ai subi d'importantes pertes financières lorsque j'ai été remercié.
Ça me fait chier de penser au fric que j'ai paumé quand ces fils de
*   putain ils m'ont foutu à la porte.*

In the summer of 1994, following a season of riots and demonstrations, a questionnaire was sent out by the then French Prime Minister, Édouard Balladur, to the young people of France (especially the unemployed). It was accompanied by a letter, part of which read as follows:

On parle souvent des «jeunes», en général. On parle souvent en votre nom. Vous avez votre propre expérience, votre propre vision de la vie, votre propre conception de l'avenir, mais on ne vous demande jamais, directement, votre avis. C'est pourquoi j'ai décidé de vous consulter personnellement.

Si vous acceptez de participer à ce dialogue, votre avis sera pris en compte. Un questionnaire vous est adressé. Il sera dépouillé et analysé par un comité indépendant du Gouvernement et composé de personnalités très diverses. Vos réponses me seront communiquées . . .

. . . Il dépend de nous tous – et de vous en particulier – que la société soit plus juste, que notre pays continue à progresser, qu'il développe la solidarité et la coopération dans le monde pour venir en aide aux peuple défavorisés.

- Characterize the level of language used here, referring to specific features of grammar and vocabulary.

For the entertainment of readers of *L'Événement du jeudi*, the journalist Liliane Sichler rewrote the letter as though it had been composed by Bernard Tapie (a businessman of humble origins who at the time was prominent in Socialist Party politics) in a style more likely to appeal to francophones under the age of 25. Here is the 'translation' of the paragraph just quoted:

Moi, je vais vous dire, les discours sur «les jeunes» en général, j'en ai rien à foutre. A la télévision, dans les journaux, il y toujours des types qui causent à votre place. Pourtant moi, je le sais, les mômes, ils ont des trucs à dire. Des trucs que jamais les bureaucrates ne viennent leur demander. Il y a la galère, le chômage, mais il y a aussi les rêves. C'est pas parce que t'es né dans une cité pourrie que tu rêves pas d'avenir! J'en sais quelque chose. C'est pour ça que j'ai décidé de vous interroger perso, chacun d'entre vous.

Allez-y, c'est l'occase. Vous avez tout à gagner en répondant à mon questionnaire. Ceux qui n'aiment pas écrire, ils auront juste à taper «Tapie-jeunes» sur le minitel. Pour m'aider à bien tout piger dans vos réponses, j'ai réuni des gens qui n'ont rien à voir avec la politique. J'attends vos messages, je les lirai tous . . .

. . . On est tous dans le bain. Et ça dépend de nous tous que la société soit plus réglo, que la France soit toujours plus forte et plus sympa. Y a du pain sur la planche, chez nous et partout dans le monde.

(*L'Événement du jeudi*, 23 June 1994)

- What features of vocabulary and grammar are used here that would have been inappropriate in the original?

- What elements of content have been changed, and what unchanged correspondences can you find between the two versions?

■■ What overall effects of language are being sought in this version of the Prime Minister's letter?

Spontaneous or contrived?

The pastiche just quoted is inevitably somewhat 'forced' – a stylistic exercise, not a genuine letter. More authentically colloquial are the following excerpts from claims sent to insurance companies after traffic accidents (the original spelling and punctuation are preserved).

(a) La citroën avait priorité c'est un fait, mais je ne l'ai pas vu, d'ailleurs à la façon qu'il conduisait on voyait bien que la priorité il savait pas ce que c'était la preuve que si çà aurait été le contraire (une auto qu'aurait venu par la gauche) il l'emboutissait pareil. Donc il n'y a pas de motif de s'arrêter à cette question de priorité à laquelle vous donnez tant d'importance.

(b) Je suis entré dans la terrasse d'un café avec ma 2 CV, comme il y avait beaucoup de choses j'en ai cassé beaucoup aussi. Il y avait personne ça fait toujours ça de moins (voir la liste à peu près):
– 3 tables (pas tellement bien)
– des chaises (en mauvais état)
– un tonneau paint en rouge dans quoi il y avait un ganre d'arbuste (le tonneau est pas récupérable, mais l'arbuste si)
– il y avait aussi un peu de verrerie mais des bouteilles il y en avait pas sans ça c'était pire. Le restant que j'ai eu en dommager c'est pas au café, c'est la grille d'un jardin public qui est à la commune, c'est comme le banc et le feu rouge . . .
– il y avait un chien aussi mais il s'est sauvé assez vite et on l'a pas revu il a du rien avoir et on ne sait pas à qui c'est, ça a pas arrangé ma 2 CV non plus et elle est pas finie de payée.
    En déplorant énergiquement je vous salue avec dévouement.

PS: ma femme a été commotionnée et aura, surement des cicatrices à la figure mais c'est rien le docteur y a mis des infectants.

Such pieces of writing are obviously strongly influenced by spoken usage (*français populaire*, specifically). They also point to less than perfect mastery of the written medium.

■ What grammatical and lexical evidence can you find for both these points?

■■ Together with a number of other similar excerpts, these texts made up a humorous article in a weekly news magazine (*L'Événement du jeudi*, 28 May 1992). What do you think readers were expected to find amusing about them, and what role would language have played in this?

Now, unlike the earlier pastiche by L. Sichler (see p. 157), the two extracts from insurance claims give the appearance of having been 'thrown together' with little if any preparation or editing.

■ Can you illustrate this?

Though unusual in written texts, spontaneity (or unpreparedness), is as striking a feature of spoken language as are colloquialisms. It is characterized by slips of the tongue, grammatical errors, sudden changes of construction, and a general looseness of organization which makes it, for example, very difficult to divide the transcription of a spontaneous text neatly into sentences. You will have noticed such features in the first excerpt in this chapter (p. 154): they serve to distinguish authentic spoken French from the kind of artificial colloquial seen in the Sichler text and which is more and more often encountered in the press and in advertising (see Chapter 10). Here are two further excerpts which differ significantly in respect of spontaneity.

(a) J'ai une copine au journal, ça va pas, ça va pas bien du tout. Tragique! Une crème, cette fille, douce, indulgente, gentille. Très cool, très relax, très calme. Un lac, une mer étale, jamais de vagues. Oui et alors? Qu'est-ce qu'elle a? Ben, elle a ça, bon caractère, et ça ne se pardonne pas. Non, sérieux, contrairement à ce qu'on croit, c'est pas le stress qui est fatal, c'est la sérénité. Pour les femmes, attention! Les hommes, eux, plus ils se contrôlent, mieux ils se portent. D'où je le tire? D'une étude menée pendant onze ans à l'université du Michigan. Il en ressort que sa colère faut la piquer, pas la rentrer, si on veut couper à une mort prématurée.

(b) Bon ben, j'raconte une histoire, quand j'étais... pendant les vacances. Alors c'est une fois j'ai été chez mes cousins. I'neigeait i'neigeait. Puis heu le soir j'm'amus ... heu j'm'amusais dans la neige avec mes soeurs et mes cous ... et ma cousine aussi, et puis alors heu je m'suis enfoncée dans la neige et puis, y a une épine qui m'est rentré dans le doigt – alors heu le lendemain quand j'suis le lendemain mon papa a essayé de m'l'ôter l'épine, mais elle elle était trop enfoncée alors i'pouvait pas m'l'enfonc i' pouvait pas me, l'ôter – alors heu mon papa m'a laissée comme ça i'm'a fait un pansement, puis le lendemain i'm'a emmenée à l'hôpital, alors heu, je heu mon papa a demandé à quelqu'un de l'hôpital pour me faire soigner alors heu c'est un monsieur qui m'a soignée i'm'a couchée sur un lit roulant.

■ Identify colloquial features of grammar in each of (a) and (b).

Apart from *bon ben* and *heu*, there seem to be no particularly colloquial features in the vocabulary of (b). Text (a), on the other hand, contains several examples.

■ What colloquial features of lexis can you find in (a)?

In spite of this, (b) seems more 'colloquial' than (a) in terms of its overall style and organization.

■ In (b), find as many features of unpreparedness as you can.

Such features are lacking in (a). What (a) does show, on the other hand, are words that are carefully arranged in rhythmic groups of three, and the systematic use of a question-and-answer format to introduce points.

■ Can you locate these?

In fact (a) is from an article by a fashionable columnist in *Le Monde* (C. Sarraute, 22 November 1990), whereas (b) is from an interview with a 10-year-old (CREDIF 1969: 39). Although (b) contains fewer colloquialisms of vocabulary than (a), the ones it does contain (e.g. *heu*) are particularly characteristic of spontaneous or unprepared discourse. It should be contrasted with the following *imitation* of children's discourse from a work of fiction:

Papa, alors, a regardé Rex et il lui a gratté la tête, comme il me fait à moi, quelquefois. «C'est vrai qu'il a l'air en bonne santé, ce petit chien», il a dit papa, et puis, il a tendu l'autre main et il a dit: «La patte, donne la papatte, allons la papatte, donne!» et Rex lui a donné la papatte et puis il lui a léché la main et puis il s'est gratté l'oreille, il était drôlement occupé, Rex. Papa, il rigolait et puis il m'a dit: «Bon, attends moi ici, je vais essayer d'arranger ça avec ta mère», et il est entré dans la maison. Il est chouette papa! Pendant que papa arrangeait ça avec maman, je me suis amusé avec Rex, qui s'est mis à faire le beau et puis comme je n'avais rien à lui donner à manger, il s'est remis à gratter son oreille, il est terrible, Rex!

(Sempé-Goscinny 1960: 52)

■■ In what ways is the 'contrived' nature of this excerpt revealed?

Dialogues can show the same kinds of contrast between prepared and unprepared discourse:

– *Conversation in the street*

A: André! Fais attention, mon vieux! Veux-tu te mettre sous les roues de cette auto?

B: (*à bicyclette*). Oh, il n'y a pas de mal. Je lui ai donné un mètre pour me doubler.

A: Que fais-tu ce soir?

B: Je ne sais pas. Ce n'est pas encore décidé. Je crois que mon père veut sortir après le dîner, et que je l'accompagne, mais je ne sais pas où.

A: Iras-tu au théâtre, peut-être?

B: Je n'en suis pas sûr. Ce sera au théâtre ou à l'Opéra, bien sûr, puisque mon père aime tellement l'opéra.

A: Mais est-ce que ce sont vraiment de bons chanteurs cette semaine-ci? Ils présentent «Le Barbier de Séville», je crois.

– *Discussion about travel*

A: C'est combien le bateau, vous qui savez, c'est combien le bateau pour aller en Angleterre?

B: Ça dépend d'combien de temps tu restes.

A: Une journée, ou deux quoi, ché pas.

B: Ah bah si tu restes deux jours, à ce moment-là t'as l'aller-retour en trois jours qu'est intéressant.

C: Deux cent cinquante balles ou un truc comme ça.

B: Trois jours c'est trois jours le minimum en fait, enfin t'as l'aller-retour dans la journée mais ça c'est pas intéressant tu peux pas aller à Londres, si tu prends l'aller-retour dans la journée t'as pas l'temps d'aller à Londres.

C: Si, si, pas d'problème, moi j'lai déjà fait.

A: T'as déjà fait?

C: Tu prends l'car l'matin à neuf heures . . . à six heures et demie.

B: Tu passes que quatre heures ou six heures à Londres.

C: T'arrives à, à dix heures si ça s'passe bien, dix heures, dix heures et demie, tu repars le soir à six heures du soir, quoi.

A: Ça te fait six heures là-bas, quoi.

C: Oui, c'est suffisant.

B: Ça dépend de ce que t'as à faire.

One of these is from a genuine conversation (Hauchecorne 1996), the other from a language-learning manual (Arnold 1968: 9).

■■ Say which is which, and comment on the differences between the two, referring to overall organization as well as to grammar and vocabulary.

Variation and context

It should be clear by now that situational factors provide a context within which particular utterances will be appropriate or inappropriate. The following sentences contain elements which would be unnatural in the contexts indicated.

–   (*Autograph hunter to world-famous author*) Monsieur, voulez-vous signer ma copie de votre bouquin, s'il vous plaît?

–   (*Car salesman to customer*) Cette nouvelle Renault est une excellente bagnole, Madame.

–   (*Mugger to victim*) Filez-moi votre fric, ou je vous assène un coup.

–   (*Teenager A to teenager B*) Dis, si on se rendait à la disco ce soir?

(*Reply of teenager B*) Cela m'est indifférent.

– (*Tour de France spectator A to spectator B*) Qui va emporter cette étape, à ton avis?

(*Reply of spectator B*) Ma foi, je ne saurais te le dire.

■■ Explain the anomalies, and then put them right.

The importance of such conventions, and the consternation that can result if they are flouted, underlie the following guidelines about correct address forms proposed by the humorist Roger Alexandre. The setting is an imaginary firm whose chairman (*président-directeur général*) is a M. Dugommeau:

Postons-nous à la porte de Dugommeau et notons les diverses façons dont ses visiteurs l'abordent. Nous en relevons six.

Monsieur le directeur. C'est le degré 0 de la familiarité. A ce niveau, le triple prosternement ne serait pas déplacé.

Monsieur tout court. Degré 1: la glace est rompue, mais l'ambiance reste frisquette.

Monsieur Dugommeau. Degré 2: là, on sent pointer un réchauffement de température.

Dugommeau. Degré 3: on arrive à une vraie familiarité.

Charles-Édouard. Degré 4: là, on se retrouve vraiment entre proches . . .

Doudou (Charlie, Coco, ma vieille, etc.) Degré 5 et arrêtons-nous là: au-delà, on sortirait sans doute du cadre de ce livre à vocation managériale.

Il est évident que vous ne devez pas faire intervenir le tutoiement avant d'avoir vérifié que vous avez accès au minimum au degré 3, et de préférence au 4 (Charles-Édouard). Au lieu de: «Monsieur le directeur, votre dernière note est sublime», vous pourrez alors déclarer: «Charles-Édouard, ta note est un peu confuse.» Ou: «Doudou, on comprend que dalle à ton galimatias».

(Alexandre 1991: 28)

■ What are the implications of each of the italicized address-forms?

■■ How do these tie in with other features of language, including the choice between *tu* and *vous* ?

Alexandre also points out (1991: 29) that *Salut, Francis*! *Ça boume, tous tes business?* would probably be an inappropriate greeting for an employee to address to the company chairman on encountering him in the lift.

■ How many contextually inappropriate features can you find in the sentence just quoted?

Here are some further greetings or *salutations*;

bonjour; à demain; à plus; à tout à l'heure; adieu; allô; au revoir; bonne continuation; ciao; enchanté; salut; bonne fin de repas; bonne nuit

And here are some contexts:

(a) diner to companions after being called away urgently
(b) boss saying goodbye to employee
(c) customer on leaving a shop
(d) job applicant at end of interview
(e) old lady taking leave of teatime hosts
(f) one colleague to another at end of work
(g) orator to deceased at funeral
(h) shopkeeper to departing customer
(i) teenager to friends at exit from disco
(j) night porter to hotel guest.

■ Which of the greetings would make no sense in some or all of these 'leave-taking' situations (wrong literal meaning)?

■ Of those that do make sense, which wouldn't fit certain of the situations because they have the wrong 'extralinguistic' implications? Specify these.

The following episode is from an account of classroom life in a 'difficult' school in a Paris suburb. Even rowdy 12-year-olds are evidently sensitive to the relationship between social context and level of language.

La classe bouillonne.
«Monsieur . . . y a eu un problème. La prof d'histoire, elle a dit *ta gueule* à Eric.

– C'est vrai, elle a pas à nous parler comme si qu'on était des chiens!

– Y en a plein qui sont choqués, franchement, ça s'fait pas!»

Je reconstitue l'incident avec la classe. Eric parlait sous le nez de ma collègue. Cinq *tais-toi!* crescendo n'ont pas pu faire cesser son bavardage. Je le connais, Eric, toujours assis au premier rang, ne tenant pas en place, n'écoutant jamais . . .

Excédée, ma collègue eût pu vociférer un *Ta gueule!* familier, certes, mais compréhensible. Or, j'apprends qu'elle a réussi à rester dans le seul registre de langue que sa fonction professorale autorisait, et qu'elle a pris soin de dire:

«Dans ta langue: *Ta gueule!*»

Une application grandeur nature de la classique leçon sur les niveaux de langage.

SOUTENU: *Auriez-vous l'amabilité de mettre fin à votre bavardage?*

COURANT: *Tais-toi, s'il te plaît!*

FAMILIER: *Ta gueule!*

(Seguin and Teillard 1996: 154–5)

■■ Why are the pupils shocked, and how justified are they?

Shifting between levels

The increasing receptiveness of the written code to colloquialisms (seen in one or two of the above excerpts, and discussed further in Chapter 10) means that writers are more and more prone to obtain effects of humour, irony and innuendo by switching backwards and forwards between colloquial, standard and formal levels.

Here is a typical example from a work of fiction. Note that the colloquialisms are not all contained in the dialogue, and the more literary features are not confined to the narration.

The action takes place in the imaginary and insalubrious Paris suburb of La Décharge. Colourful local characters Juju, Renée and L'Artisse are sheltering the murderer of two policemen, whose colleagues have just arrived in force to investigate.

Les flics étaient à La Décharge. Les flics cernaient La Décharge. A chaque coin de rue se tenait un camion de CRS. Il y avait des voitures radio, des chiens policiers, des flics à képi de luxe et des flics en civil. Il y avait des journalistes et des armées de flics, un quatorze juillet de flics, le grand bal de la Police.

– Tout ça pour un seul mec, rigola Juju qui, entre Renée et L'Artisse, contemplait de ses carreaux le déploiement bleu sombre des forces de l'ordre. L'Artisse gloussa:

– Oui, mais quel mec, comme tu dis. Un homme. Un homme qui a supprimé de la surface de la terre deux des collègues de ces messieurs.

– Ça, ils peuvent pas le lui pardonner, fit Renée.

C'était à l'aube que les policiers avaient investi La Décharge, empêchant même les ouvriers de partir au travail. Ils avaient jeté le quartier sous les mailles d'acier de leur épervier.

(Fallet 1956: 73)

- Identify the various levels here.

■■ Work out the effects of shift, and specify the extralinguistic features which trigger off the use of one or other language level. In particular, what information does the narrator's choice convey about his attitude to the police?

This excerpt is from a fairly mainstream novel which is not noticeably adventurous in its use of language. Many francophone writers of crime fiction proper make more extensive use of colloquial vocabulary – in particular the variety known as *argot*.

Originally, this term referred to the secret vocabulary of marginal social groups – criminals in particular – and it is still used in this sense (*argot traditionnel*). However, many elements of *argot* have found their way into more general use, and have accordingly lost their 'secrecy'. Hence a broader sense of the term (*argot commun*) in which *argot* simply refers to the most colloquial range of the vocabulary.

Many *argotique* items (both traditional and 'common') have gone out of real-life use altogether, but remain a stock-in-trade of writers of detective stories (who on occasion supply explanatory footnotes for the most unfamiliar terms). Here is an example of level-shift involving a blend of *argot traditionnel* and *argot commun* (underlined) together with an admixture of *français soigné* (italicized). This particular best-selling author's books are language games as much as they are adventures.

The setting is an imaginary island off Cornwall. Hero and narrator Commissaire San-Antonio, pursued by a gang of criminals, and having temporarily hidden in a fish lorry, seeks refuge in a village school.

Intriguée, la maîtresse d'école s'avance. Mais je <u>fouette</u> tellement la merluche qu'elle stoppe à trois pas de moi. Je lui <u>fais mater ma brêmouze de poulardin</u>.
– J'appartiens à la police française et *des gens de mauvaise mentalité sont à mes trousses*, miss, pouvez-vous me cacher et, ensuite, alerter mes confrères britanniques?

Elle <u>défrime</u> ma carte; *vainc sa panique olfactive* et *s'empresse* d'aller <u>délourder</u> une porte basse, au fond du couloir.
– Mettez-vous ici!

C'est le placard à balais, seaux, combustibles, etc.

J'engouffre. Elle <u>relourde</u> au verrou.

L'odeur du charbon se met à concurrencer celle de mes <u>fringues</u>, mais elle abandonne vite la partie pour cause d'insuffisance. Si les <u>truands</u> qui me coursent <u>se pointent</u> dans l'école, <u>sûr qu'</u>ils me <u>retapisseront</u> au fumet. Justement, un léger quart de <u>plombe</u> plus tard, j'entends <u>discutailler dans le coinceteau</u> . . .

(San-Antonio 1974: 165–6)

fouetter: sentir; *mater*: regarder; *brême*, *brêmouze*: carte; *poulet*, *poulaga*, *poulardin*: policier en civil; *défrimer*: regarder avec attention; *délourder*: ouvrir une porte; *fringues*: vêtements; *truand*: malfaiteur, criminel; *se pointer*: arriver; *retapisser*: reconnaître.

■ Often the meaning of words in this kind of writing can be guessed from their context, or indeed from their appearance. What do the following seem to mean?

plombe; *discutailler*; *coinceteau*.

■■ Consult native French-speakers in order to ascertain how many of the underlined items are in current general use.

■■ What are the effects in this excerpt of the switches to formal language?

■■■ There are many more grammatical and lexical markers of formality/informality in French than can be mentioned here. Find some, and make a classification of them along the formal–colloquial scale.

■■■ Traditionally the most colloquial levels (notably *français populaire* and *français vulgaire*) have been associated with the lower social classes, whereas *français soigné* and *français littéraire* are regarded as a preserve of the bourgeoisie and aristocracy. How valid nowadays is this correlation between register and class?

Further reading

The kinds of variation dealt with in this chapter are extensively exemplified in Batchelor and Offord (1982), Muller (1985) and Offord (1990). For discussion and evaluation of the assumptions behind the various classifications, see Chapter 2 of Sanders (1993). Gadet (1992), in the *Que sais-je?* series, is a handy account of popular and familiar usage, and the relationship between informal and formal French is discussed in Lodge (1993). Useful dictionaries of colloquial French include Bernet and Rézeau (1989) and Caradec (1989).

•　　•　　•

Innovation, conservation and defence

Spontaneous innovation

'Ça bouge en français'

Not only is there a great deal of long-standing variation between different levels of French, as the last chapter has shown, but the language is currently undergoing quite far-reaching transformations which are adding to the variety. 'Ça bouge en français', as people sometimes say.

The present chapter will focus on three innovative aspects.

- The emergence of a new style of *argot*.
- The fact that this, together with older colloquialisms, is more and more often finding its way into written usage (once very largely a preserve of *bon usage*).
- The way in which the written language itself has been developing an increasingly prevalent 'technocratic' style, which is having its effect on spoken usage.

Le parler 'jeune'

There is nothing new about the coining of colloquialisms: each generation of speakers makes its own contribution to the vocabulary, and the actual methods of coining words change little over time. Today, though, the influence of the media gives many innovations much wider currency than would have been the case a few decades ago, though most new items still become dated very rapidly.

If older speakers are usually the innovators as far as the vocabulary of such areas as science, technology or business is concerned, then current colloquial innovations owe much to the inventiveness of younger people. The age group is hard to delimit precisely: it seems to centre on adolescents, but extends at least as far as speakers in their mid-twenties.

The rapid turnover of many vocabulary items from generation to generation is evoked as follows in a collection of such items published in 1994 by the journalists Eliane Girard and Brigitte Kernel, and intended to provide enlightenment for mystified parents.

Vos parents disaient: «C'est un spectacle formidable, avec des comédiens extraordinaires.»

Vous disiez: «C'est un show vachement cool, avec des acteurs super.»

Vos enfants disent: «C'est top, comme show, avec des teuracs wizz, j'te dis pas.»

(Girard and Kernel 1994: cover)

■ Which age group is being addressed here?

■ The first of these three (invented) sentences is the closest to *bon usage*: can you specify in what respects?

The third quotation («*C'est top, comme show, avec des teuracs wizz, j'te dis pas*») gives some insight into current coinages and their origin. *Top*, *show* and *wizz* are, of course, anglicisms.

■■ But are they all used in quite the way an anglophone would use them? That is, are they straightforward borrowings from English, or are they examples of *franglais* (English words adapted to French usage)?

Teuracs is an example of *verlan*, a way of disguising words by inverting their syllables which has long been a feature of schoolchildren's slang. The term *verlan* itself is the result of applying this process to the expression (*à*) *l'envers* ('back-to-front').

■ Can you 'deverlanize' *teuracs* and recover the original (standard) term?

J'te dis pas isn't to be taken literally: it's the kind of phrase used at all levels of spoken language to cover up hesitations and/or to establish rapport with the listener.

■ What would a *bon usage* equivalent be?

Anglicisms and *verlan* are just two sources of new vocabulary. Also noteworthy are the use made of prefixes and suffixes, and the frequent abbreviation of words.

For further illustration, the two journalists mentioned above devised the following highly concentrated paragraph of what they call *le langage ado* (i.e. *adolescent*), together with a paraphrase of it in standard French.

173

Janet est une meuf giga. Hyprabien sapée, classe, pas vulgos, pas trop chébran. En plus elle en a dans la teuté, j'te dirai. Je le crois pas comment elle fait marcher son keum . . . Mais coolos il se laisse faire, no problem. J'te dis pas je le comprends! Une meuf comme ça c'est du tonbé, c'est juste good luck d'être béton dessus. J'te raconte pas les autres keums! I'zont aucune chance!

Janet est une jolie fille. Elégante, elle a de la classe et ne montre jamais aucune vulgarité, pas plus qu'elle n'essaie d'être branchée. En plus elle est intelligente. Ce qui est extraordinaire, c'est la façon dont elle fait marcher son petit ami à la baguette . . . Cela ne lui pose aucun problème, c'est un garçon très gentil. Je le comprends, c'est sûr! Une fille comme elle, c'est du solide, et il a bien de la chance d'être l'heureux élu. Tant pis pour les autres!

(Girard and Kernel 1994: 26)

- Are *no problem* and *good luck* straightforward anglicisms or examples of *franglais*?

Coolos consists of an anglicism, to which has been added a suffix much used in this type of language for giving a novel form to adjectives.

- Divide *coolos* into its two parts. Does the suffix appear to change the basic meaning in any way?

- Find another occurrence in the paragraph of the same suffix. Is there any effect on the meaning in this case?

Hyprabien illustrates the use of an intensifier prefix.

- Say what the prefix is, give its approximate meaning, and think of some other prefixes with similar meaning (specifying which language level they belong to).

Note also the way *classe* is used as an adjective instead of as a noun. This style of language has something of a penchant for reclassifying parts of speech like this (more examples later).

The excerpt contains six further examples of *verlan*, based respectively on:

béton branché femme mec tête tomber

- Identify the *verlan* words in the excerpt, and insert each of them opposite its corresponding 'translation'.

- Words that are already colloquial can also be 'verlanized'. Find some examples from among the above.

■■ Which *verlan* items result from a straightforward interchange of syllables (as was the case with *teuracs*), and which correspond to a more complex process which applies to words of only one syllable? Can you work out what happens in the case of these one-syllable words?

In the following excerpt (not a journalist's invention this time), Saïd, a 13-year-old *verlan* virtuoso from a Paris suburb, describes his first, rather disastrous, encounter with marijuana (*verlan* in phonetic transcription).

CHRISTOPHE (*interviewer*): Bon, on va y aller.
SAÏD: [atak] poser des questions.
C: Est-ce que t'as déjà [mefy] du [tøʃi]?
S: Ouais, t'sais regarde, j'vais t'raconter une histoire tu vas, t'es obligé, tu vas t'exploser de rire là-d'dans, on était à la [məbu] à la [ləsa] là-bas, tu vois où qu'c'est la [rime] . . . on arrive là-bas, pis tu vois j', j'savais pas qu'yz étaient en train d'[mefy] un joint . . . t'sais yz y vont tous vers le fond, j'savais pas c'que c'était tout, j'y vais, j'vois yz é . . . , t'sais y prennent du papier tabac, pis yz étaient en train de de l'[leko] . . . j'dis euh, vous êtes en train de faire un [wɛʒ]?, après y m'ont dit eh oh . . . après y m'l'ont allumé t'sais moi j'sais pas moi j'[mefy] la [garətsi] d'accord, t'sais y, j'avais [me], jamais [mefy] d'joint . . . y commencent à [mefy] tout, j'leur dis [warf] une [fəta], j'dis c'est rien ça, c'est ça euh le joint? . . . je reprends une deuxième taf, j'dis c'est ça le joint pas terrib', près y m'[sepa] la troisième [fəta], j'prends une troisième, sur ma vie j'tenais plus sur mes cannes j'étais [sakom] j'suis [betɔ̃] sur la chaise et [sakom] [terpa], ah oh ouais j'étais complètement . . .

(Mela 1988: 67–8)

- The meaning of most of the *verlan* items here should be obvious enough, except perhaps for the equivalents of (in order of occurrence) *tu n'as qu'à* (*t'as qu'à*), *shit*, *boum*, *cigarette*, *fais voir*, *par terre*. Can you locate these, and identify the others?

It should be clear from this excerpt that, alongside all the innovations, young teenagers like Saïd make extensive use of perfectly traditional colloquialisms of vocabulary and grammar. Indeed, this particular speaker tends to use *verlan* only when telling stories, as is pointed out by the linguist who recorded his speech patterns, and who comments:

> Saïd prend un plaisir évident à raconter ses «petites histoires», à manier un langage dont il est le maître, à égarer ses auditeurs dans un univers à l'envers ... Cette fonction poétique est peut-être aussi importante que la fonction référentielle. C'est là que réside sans doute la véritable richesse du verlan.
>
> (Mela 1988: 70)

■■ What do you think is meant here by the 'fonction poétique' of *verlan*?

Other investigations into the use of *verlan* show that the more deprived the environment of its users, the more often it is likely to be heard. A lot of it originates on run-down estates (*cités*) on the edges of large towns (such as the one lived in by Saïd), and this applies to other features of adolescent language as well. The following account by a teacher testifies to its frequent incomprehensibility:

> En sortant de chez moi ... je trouve Samir, membre éminent de la sous-culture des rues – excellent locuteur de *verlan* par la même occasion – que j'ai eu comme élève et avec qui j'entretiens depuis le départ une relation à la fois amicale et très conflictuelle. Il est adossé au mur de l'immeuble C de la place Joliot-Curie. Me voyant arriver de loin, il appelle un de ses copains qui traîne devant la barre «Renoir» et se met à lui parler *verlan* comme une mitraillette, ostensiblement et tout en me regardant venir avec un sourire narquois. J'arrive tout juste à saisir qu'il parle de moi et dans des termes qui semblent péjoratifs.
>
> (Lepoutre 1994: 7)

■■ What is the role of such a 'secret language' in the relationship between young people and authority figures?

Obviously *verlan* provides a powerful reinforcement of peer-group solidarity and identity. To become a proficient speaker is to go through an important initiation process (Saïd and Samir have been spectacularly successful in this respect), and it is noticeable that its use usually decreases once an individual's adolescent years are over.

■■ *'Le «parler des cités», passeport et refuge'*. This is the title of a newspaper article about these language varieties (*Le Monde*, 18 January 1996). Can you explain it?

■■ What parallels are there between *verlan* and the criminal *argot* referred to in Chapter 9?

■■ The vocabulary of secret languages like *verlan* shows a rapid turnover of items. Why should this be?

■■■ *Verlan* as such is in no way a new phenomenon: it goes back decades, if not centuries. But what social factors have contributed to its greatly increased use by working-class teenagers in recent years?

'Faux jeune', 'français branché' and the renewal of the written language

The paragraph quoted earlier from Girard and Kernel's book contains only one example of more traditional *argot*: *sapée* ('dressed'). But a comparison with the language use of a speaker like Saïd shows how artificial such 'demonstration paragraphs' can be. Not only are the innovations more densely packed than they would be in real life – some of the expressions listed by the authors are not even encountered in actual usage (at least not any more). This point was emphasized by one of their reviewers:

> En direct dans «Coucou c'est nous», [C. Dechavanne] a demandé à son jeune, très jeune public s'il connaissait les expressions glanées au fil des pages. Malheureusement non. C'est à désespérer. Les jeunes ne causent pas comme des jeunes. Ils ne se «ruinent pas le groin». Rien ne «les trône», pas même «une portion de gland». Ils ne goûtent guère «la taupe qui pointe son nez». A moins qu'ils n'aient attentivement lu Frédéric Dard (né en 1921). Le faux jeune les aura égarés.
>
> Le faux jeune? C'est parler comme un jeune quand on ne l'est plus. Une faute de syntaxe ici, un néologisme là, le style faux jeune envahit le paysage, alors que la France vieillit . . .

> ... Le sabir des jeunes ne se laisse pas apprivoiser. Il reste toutefois possible d'en pêcher quelques spécimens. A consommer rapidement. Il en va du vocabulaire comme du poisson: il ne reste pas frais longtemps.
>
> (Philippe Vandel, *Le Nouvel Observateur*, 17 March 1994)

Coucou c'est nous is a popular television programme for teenagers, presented by Christophe Dechavanne. The expressions quoted here are all taken from Girard and Kernel's collection. Frédéric Dard is the author of the classic Commissaire San-Antonio stories mentioned in Chapter 9.

■ What general warning about published collections of fashionable *argot* is implied in Vandel's comments?

■■ What does he mean by '*le faux jeune*', and what is paradoxical about it?

■■ What is the significance of his reference to Frédéric Dard?

The conversion of *le langage ado* by media and entertainment people into a kind of art form has had two main results. Elements of 'youth language' have begun to enter the usage of older generations (Vandel's *faux jeune*), and it is more and more often encountered in written texts, alongside the traditional colloquialisms which have also been making inroads into this medium. Together with an admixture of more abstract and 'intellectual' items contributed by the 'chattering classes', there results the fashionable amalgam known as *le français branché* (*branché* literally means 'plugged in', as applied to electrical equipment). The regionalist writer Claude Duneton comments as follows on the way the use of this has spread, as compared with the *argots* of previous eras:

> Il y a toujours eu un langage à la mode, avec ses engouements, ses tics, ses maniérismes ... La différence, aujourd'hui – la véritable nouveauté sans doute – c'est que les mots nouveaux ne courent plus longuement le ruisseau, ni les salons, ni les bordels, avant de pénétrer dans l'usage. Ils croissent dans les banlieues, dans les zones bruyantes de la musique rock, se fortifient dans les cours d'art dramatique, dans le show-biz et dans la pub; ils circulent tout de suite dans les foules socialement hybrides qui hantent les concerts rock, bruissent dans les salles de rédaction, et de là sifflent sur les ondes jusque dans les chaumières en béton du pays tout entier.
>
> (Preface to Merle 1989: 7–8)

■■ According to this, what aspects of contemporary culture seem to favour the rapid dissemination of new language varieties, and what channels are available?

Some examples follow that show the effects of these various kinds of innovation on the traditional written language. The following categories of usage are illustrated:

(a) standard
(b) literary
(c) traditional colloquialisms
(d) *langage jeune* or *faux jeune*
(e) fashionable intellectual items
(f) *franglais*.

■ In a few cases, an indication is given as to which of the above categories (a)–(f) are present. Specify exactly which words or expressions correspond to which categories.

■■ In the other cases you should decide for yourself which categories are present and say how they are exemplified.

JOURNALISTIC USAGE

1 Bouquins-vacances: la sélection des manageurs (*L'Expansion*)
 (a, c, f)
2 Pour trois mille balles, cette escapade fait du bien. Les pensions honnêtes vous attendent dans le quartier près de la gare. Pour manger, évitez les restos clinquants pour ne rentrer que dans les«cervezerias», restos popus aux menus à 1 000 pesetas (*Actuel*).
 (a, c)
3 . . . aussi nombreux soient-ils et le fussent-ils plus encore, c'est eux qui ont tort (*F. Cavanna*).
 (a, b, c)
4 Suffisait que la télévision acceptât de jouer le jeu. Elle accepta, la salope (*F. Cavanna*).
5 A 20 ans, il avait plaqué la fac de droit pour lancer, avec des copains, une société de multiservices aux entreprises. A 33 ans . . . il a découvert un secteur en plein boom et pas encore structuré: celui des expos et salons. Ce sera son créneau (*L'Expansion*).

ADVERTISING

1 La Sécu c'est bien, en abuser ça craint (*social security poster*)
(a, c, d)

2 Maxwell qualité filtre: pas la peine d'en mettre un max (*Maxwell House coffee*)
(c, d)

3 Soyez pas nuls, filez vos globules (*Blood transfusion appeal*)
(c, d)

4 Quand je bouge je bus (*Provincial bus operator*)
(d)

5 Quand y'en a plus, y'en a encore (*Palmolive*)

6 Un jour sans Bic c'est la barbe (*Bic razors*)

7 Europe 1, c'est la pêche (*Europe 1*)

8 La France, nous, on l'aime! (*Referendum poster*)

9 Fuck le sida! (*Safer sex poster*)

10 Ne disons pas «Super bons ces bonbecs»;
Disons plutôt «Ces friandises sont exquises» (*Sweets by La Vosgienne*)

■■ Why should this sort of language be popular with advertisers?

■■ What influence would you expect advertisements to have in opening up the written language to colloquial influence?

EXAMPLE FROM A NOVEL

By the compiler of a celebrated dictionary of *français branché*. At a crowded concert, the narrator approaches an old friend turned pop star.

> Je coupe un symposium de psycho-bilieux cyberpunks post-new-wave mâtinés cochon d'Inde, et j'arrive dans la proche banlieue de l'idole. Je le heurte très légèrement du coude au moment où il explique que «vraiment la télé en ce moment, c'est galère-que-je-vous-raconte pas», ce qui me permet de lui lancer en passant un «pardon-tiens-quelle-surprise-comment-tu-vas-toi» pas piqué des hannetons. Le Morrison tourne la tête vers moi, me fait un clin d'oeil en me tapant léger sur l'épaule, et m'envoie: «Ça roule, et toi, Rich'! On se téléphone, hein?»
>
> (Merle 1991: 147)

■■■ Make a survey of any French-language newspapers, periodicals and/or contemporary novels that you have access to, trying to spot examples of this kind of usage. Which publications, and which sections of them, seem to be the most hospitable to *le langage branché*, and why?

The administrative/technocratic style

It is not only in colloquial French that traditional and newly coined items are to be found side by side. Already in the 1930s, a tendency was emerging which, half a century later, was to develop beyond anything imagined at that time. The following comment on contemporary trends, for example, appeared in the daily newspaper *Le Temps* in February 1933:

> ... dans un rapport présenté à l'assemblée générale, des ingénieurs écrivent ceci: «La pluviosité, tout en ayant été inférieure à celle de l'exercice précédent, a été néanmoins favorable ... ». Vous voulez dire: il pleut; dites: il pleut. Vous voulez dire: il a plu cette année moins que l'an dernier, dites: il a plu cette année moins que l'an dernier. Mais «il a plu moins que l'an dernier» ne ferait aucun effet dans une réunion d'actionnaires. Ils veulent un style plus savant, plus technique, plus ingénieur.
>
> *exercice*: financial year; *actionnaire*: shareholder.

■ Can you say exactly what was being objected to here?

■ In this commentator's opinion, why did the engineers express themselves in this way?

Similar in style is a notice currently on view in the public library at the Pompidou Centre in Paris:

> Toute personne quittant momentanément la bibliothèque est tenue de reprendre intégralement la file d'attente, si elle désire réintégrer les lieux.

■ What does this mean?

■■ Attempt to translate it into English, using the same level of language.

The level used in such examples is undoubtedly formal. However, as we have just seen, this was not enough to stop commentators criticizing it fifty years ago (the writer quoted on p. 181 was a novelist and a member of the Académie), and it is still frowned upon by many today. Just as there is more than one kind of colloquial (modern youth language contrasts with traditional *argot*, for instance), so formal 'administrative-technocratic' usage has a very different feel from formal literary language, and evokes very different reactions. Though originating in specialist circles, it is found more and more often in material intended for the general reader, and for this reason is a quite significant language variety.

Here is a longer example showing some of the typical features of this type of formal writing. The excerpt comes from an expensive 'coffee-table book' on the geography of France.

L'URBANISATION EN REGION PARISIENNE

L'une des difficultés qui subsistent en termes de qualité de vie urbaine est liée à la densité du tissu urbain: si le niveau général de la pollution atmosphérique a pu être notablement réduit, il reste que les deux tiers des résidents de Paris et de la petite couronne habitent à plus d'un kilomètre du moindre espace vert. A la périphérie, mille hectares d'espace libre sont encore consommés chaque année par l'urbanisation . . .

La forte minéralisation du paysage parisien n'est sans doute pas l'une des moindres raisons qui, conjuguées à l'exiguïté des logements et à la médiocrité des équipements collectifs, expliquent l'étonnante propension des Parisiens à s'évader de leur ville et à envahir chaque fin de semaine les espaces environnants, parfois fort éloignés: manifestation peut-être la plus évidente, pour le plus grand nombre, de l'intensité des relations d'interdépendance entre la capitale et les régions voisines.

(Pumain *et al.* 1990: 130)

petite couronne: inner ring of Paris suburbs.

■■ Using the first paragraph for background information, explain as concisely and simply as you can the meaning of the second paragraph.

Here are three expressions from the text, together with a less formal indication of the meaning of each.

la forte minéralisation du paysage parisien	*à Paris il y a de moins en moins d'espaces verts*
l'exiguïté des logements	*les appartements parisiens sont très petits*
les espaces environnants	*la campagne*

- *Minéralisation du paysage* and *exiguïté des logements* are examples of what is sometimes called *le style nominal* (from *nom*: 'noun'). On the basis of the above examples, can you explain what this is, and can you find one or two other examples of *style nominal* in the excerpt?

- ■ Are the items listed in the righthand column exact equivalents of those on the left, or has something been 'lost in translation'?

- ■ What advantages might there be in using the more sophisticated formulations, especially as regards their connotational meaning?

Provincial town councillors are one group who are particularly fond of this style. Not long ago, in the news magazine *L'Express*, the satirical journalist Alain Schifres drew up the following list of items characteristic of what he calls *Europrovincial* – the kind of language used in publicity and other documentation by sometimes obscure local authorities with aspirations towards European status (Schifres 1991).

NE DITES PLUS . . .	MAIS DITES . . .
Industries (moche)	*Activités*
Activités (vieilli)	*Technologies*
Technologies (d'une modestie excessive)	*Hautes technologies*
Zone d'activités	*Technopôle*
Région industrielle	*Bassin d'emploi*
Région sinistrée	*Pôle de reconversion*
Zone rurale	*Pôle agroalimentaire*
Le travail en commun	*Les fertilisations croisées*
La coopération	*La synergie*
Nîmes et Montpellier ont décidé de ne plus se mettre sur la gueule	*Les deux pôles entendent travailler en synergie dans un positionnement européen*

183

Nouveau   *Innovant*
Surmonter ses handicaps   *Mettre en valeur ses atouts*

■■ How exactly is the *Europrovincial* style used in such examples to convey an optimistic and 'upbeat' outlook?

Alain Schifres is being only slightly satirical here, as is suggested by the following excerpts from genuine local authority documentation (distributed free to private homes).

First, from a report on local activities by the Picardy regional council:

> Abbeville. Ayant entrepris de conforter ses fonctions urbaines, la ville s'attache parallèlement depuis quelques années à renforcer sa vocation sportive et culturelle. Dotée d'installations sportives performantes et d'équipements culturels de qualité, elle est à même de renforcer sa polarisation sur l'ensemble de la Picardie Maritime, en visant une démarche de promotion et de communication.

■■ Think of some specific municipal projects which might serve as concrete examples illustrating such abstract phrases as:

conforter ses fonctions urbaines
renforcer sa vocation sportive et culturelle
viser une démarche de promotion et de communication.

Second, from an election leaflet produced by the *mairie* of a small town in eastern France.

L'ENJEU MUNICIPAL

En 95, il faut:

–   Avoir une stratégie offensive pour attirer des entreprises grâce à la redynamisation de l'A31 (Allemagne–Vallée du Rhône)
–   Gagner des forces ensemble avec l'intercommunalité qui doit apporter des compléments de ressources sur les territoires des communes voisines avec qui il a été créé une «Communauté de Communes».
–   Convaincre que nous sommes, dans un milieu rural soumis à la

> PAC, dégressif mais aidé avec des crédits européens, des aides
> nationales, régionales, départementales ... par des finance-
> ments croisés efficaces qui doublent ou triplent le bon usage des
> impôts locaux et convaincre que ce monde rural restera un
> espace d'avenir et de qualité.   -
> – Continuer d'avoir une MAIRIE TRANSPARENTE où une équipe
>   honnête travaille à construire une Communauté plus efficace et
>   prospère.

PAC: politique agricole commune.

■■ What difficulties might the average householder have with such a
document?

This kind of discourse has been the object of a good deal of hostile
criticism as well as straightforward satire. For example:

> C'est une langue de pouvoir. Pouvoir de celui qui la possède sur celui
> qui l'ignore. Pouvoir de le séduire, parfois, de l'épater, souvent, de le
> faire taire, toujours. Le malheureux qui n'a que les mots de tous les
> jours ne peut qu'acquiescer. Il n'a rien à opposer au discours qui lui
> tiennent les initiés.
>
> (Huyghes 1991: 13)

■■ What is this commentator (a sociologist) concerned about, and do
you think his concerns are justified?

Perhaps not surprisingly, it is quite possible for technocratic language to
pass from writing into conversation – especially in the broadcast media,
where it is sometimes accompanied by a scattering of colloquialisms.

(a) 'Ça dépend de plein de paramètres' (*Young racing cyclist in TV
    interview*).
(b) 'L'enjeu [du match] est assez valorisant pour que chaque joueur y
    mette le maximum' (*Radio football commentary*).
(c) 'Je dois refaire une structure mentale' (*Imprisoned mass murderer
    interviewed on radio*).

■ Identify different styles and levels here.

■■ Explain – if you can – the meanings of these quotations.

185

■■ Attempt to give, in half a dozen lines, a characterization of 'administrative-technocratic language'.

■■■ Find out from francophone friends and acquaintances what they think are the main developments in the language at the present time. Do they seem happy about them?

■■■ To what extent does the distinction between written French (formal) and spoken French (informal) seem to be breaking down, and what social and technological factors might explain the erosion of the barriers? Are there parallels in English?

Further reading

Chapters 8 and 9 of Sanders (1993) deal with aspects of current developments. See also Walter (1988). A number of somewhat tongue-in-cheek accounts have appeared recently – intended for the francophone public but informative for the foreign learner. Notable among them are Girard and Kernel (1994), Merle (1989) and Philippe *et al.* (1996) for 'youth language' (including *verlan*), Huyghes (1991) for administrative-technocratic jargon, and Vandel (1992) for a range of other fashionable language-types. Certain chapters of Schifres (1990, 1994) also contain satirical evocations of trends in modern usage.

• • •

Chapter 11

Official innovation

the role of the State

A long-standing tradition

Although, as we saw in Chapter 10, the French language is continually evolving 'of its own accord', there is in francophone culture a long tradition of attempts by the public authorities deliberately to influence linguistic developments. (The tradition is commonly traced back to the royal ordinance issued by François I in 1539 at Villers-Cotterêts stipulating that legal and administrative documents must be drawn up in French – not in Latin or in regional languages like Occitan.) Here three recent examples of State intervention will be considered, each of which involves innovation of one sort or another – sometimes in response to demands from a section of the public, sometimes in a bid to forestall developments that are perceived as undesirable. The more overtly conservative aspects of the role of the State will be looked at in the following chapter.

Spelling reform

Given that one of the most popular televised events of recent years in France has been the final of the Championnats d'Orthographe, it is not surprising that an animated debate should have been triggered off by the (ill-fated) spelling reform proposed by the Socialist government in 1989, in response to representations made by primary-school teachers.

The main proposals are invoked in the following:

> La réforme de l'orthographe vise, en résumé, à souder les mots composés (pas tous), à rajouter et à déplacer quelques trémas, à décimer les accents circonflexes et à normaliser les anomalies . . .
> (Claude Weill, *Le Nouvel Observateur*,
> 10 December 1990)

Here are some examples of words affected:

Pre-reform	*Post-reform*
ambiguë	ambigüe
août	aout
auto-école	autoécole
boîte	boite
bonhomie	bonhommie
chariot	charriot
contre-ordre	contreordre
croque-monsieur	croquemonsieur
événement	évènement
exzéma	exéma
île	ile
imbecillité	imbecilité
je céderai	je cèderai
nénuphar	nénufar
oignon	ognon
porte-monnaie	portemonnaie
voûte	voute

■ Put each of these pairs into one or other of the four categories referred to above by Claude Weill.

■■ Say more specifically what the proposed change is, and try to justify it.

Altogether, the spelling of around 1,000 words would have been modified: this amounts to one word in ninety, with only half a dozen of the thousand most frequent items being affected. On average, in a continuous document, this would mean just one new spelling every two pages (Goosse 1991: 24–5), so only specially concocted texts would look conspicuously different.

■ Is the following pre-or post-reform, and how can you tell?

> De l'avis de nombreux Québécois, changer l'orthographe de quelque neuf-cents mots seulement ne va pas être la révolution redoutée par les traditionalistes partisans du statuquo, et qui ont tenté d'apporter leur véto à la réforme.

■■ The reform was criticized by some for not going far enough and by others for going too far. On the above evidence, how far do you think it went?

Partly because of the strength of feeling against the reform, and partly because of divisions within the French Academy (the body ultimately responsible for issuing rulings about spelling), the outcome was merely an agreement to 'let usage decide'. This amounted in practice to no reform at all. However, the national debate which was generated is of interest in its own right.

A survey carried out by the literary magazine *Lire* in March 1989 reveals some of the feelings of the members of the general French public about the spelling system of their language and the prospect of reform. (For each question there were up to 6 per cent 'don't know' responses, not indicated here.)

Trouvez-vous l'orthographe de la langue française très facile, assez facile, assez difficile ou très difficile?	Très facile	3%
	Assez facile	26%
	Assez difficile	45%
	Très difficile	25%
Seriez-vous très favorable, assez favorable, assez hostile ou très hostile à une réforme de l'orthographe?	Très favorable	12%
	Assez favorable	32%
	Assez hostile	25%
	Très hostile	25%

Pour vous, l'orthographe, est-ce ou non . . .

un art, quelque chose qui fait partie de notre culture, de notre patrimoine?	Non	10%
	Oui	86%
un des charmes de la langue française?	Non	16%
	Oui	78%
un pensum, un casse-tête inutile?	Non	83%
	Oui	12%

Seriez-vous, ou non, d'accord . . .

pour qu'on supprime les accents circonflexes?	Pas d'accord	52%
	D'accord	44%

pour que l'on supprime le doublement de consonnes?	Pas d'accord	59%
	D'accord	40%
pour qu'on supprime les traits d'union?	Pas d'accord	59%
	D'accord	37%
pour que l'on remplace les «ph» par un «f»?	Pas d'accord	63%
	D'accord	33%

Partagez-vous, ou non, chacune des opinions suivantes?

Il est possible de retoucher l'orthographe pour en supprimer quelques bizarreries et absurdités.	Non	19%
	Oui	76%
Il est impossible de réformer l'orthographe sans dénaturer la langue française.	Non	27%
	Oui	65%
Il est urgent de simplifier l'orthographe pour faciliter l'apprentissage de la langue française.	Oui	42%
	Non	54%

■■ Say what conclusions can be drawn from these responses as regards:

- the coherence of the public's viewpoint
- the lengths to which people think a reform should be taken
- any discrepancies between what is thought desirable in principle and what is thought desirable in practice.

Here are some specific criticisms of the proposals:

The literary editor of a major publishing house: «Stupide, inutile, dangereuse: c'est une entreprise qui relève de la pure démagogie, de l'esprit de Saddam Hussein» (Yves Berger, quoted in *Lire*, 182, November 1990).

Danièle Mitterrand (wife of the Socialist president): «Quand je vois le laxisme à propos de l'orthographe, je suis effondrée. Ce laxisme en entraînera d'autres. L'orthographe d'abord puis, pourquoi pas? la morale. Plus on demandera d'efforts aux enfants pour écrire correctement, plus ils seront formés et forts pour affronter le reste de la société» (quoted in *Le Quotidien de Paris*, 7 December 1990).

A well-known novelist: «Attention danger! Je ne suis pas résolument pour, ni violemment contre cette réforme de l'orthographe. Il n'en reste pas moins qu'aujourd'hui je n'en vois pas la nécessité. Je ne crois pas qu'il faille simplifier la vie. Nous sommes dans une époque qui aime réduire. L'idéologie dominante considère la masse comme un ensemble de primates. Cette réforme ... constitue un danger de crétinisation dans un univers déjà rongé par l'appauvrissement de la culture et un excès d'images que ne compensent ni la pratique de la lecture ni celle de l'écrivain. Je partage donc totalement l'opinion de ceux qui s'élèvent contre la «créolisation» de la langue, c'est-à-dire la simplification phonétique de l'alphabet» (Philippe Labro, *Lire*, 182, November 1990).

The secretary of the primary teachers' union: «Étant partisan d'une orthographe 'fonétic', je suis un peu déçu par la timidité des rectificateurs.»

Comments by various well-known literary figures, reported towards the end of 1990:

«Un exéma démange moins sans son z» (*Bernard Frank*).

«La voute n'a plus d'ogive sans son accent circonflexe» (*André Froissard*).

«Août est brûlant à cause de l'accent» (*Jean d'Ormesson*).

«Quand je lis 'fotografe' adieu la magie! Plus de petit oiseau qui sort de l'objectif. Les mots ne sont pas seulement des sons, mais aussi des idéogrammes» (*Norge*).

■■ Clearly, those opposing the reform did so for widely differing reasons. Identify the various motives.

Here are some comments from pro-reformers (*Lire*, 182, November 1990):

La coexistence de deux orthographes pendant une génération est inévitable si on ne veut pas procéder autoritairement. Tous ces changements demandent du temps. Regardez le passage des anciens aux nouveaux francs trente ans plus tard.

Les bizarreries font sans doute le bonheur des champions de dictée, mais elles rebutent le commun des mortels . . . Ceux qui sont attachés pour des raisons esthétiques ou sentimentales à l'ancienne orthographe (notamment les écrivains) pourront continuer à la pratiquer aussi longtemps qu'ils voudront.

Une réforme radicale ne serait pas acceptée. Les rectifications actuelles résultent forcément de compromis. Certains mots échappent donc aux nouvelles règles, mais peu. Les nouvelles exceptions sont limitées et plus simples à mémoriser.

Les Italiens et les Espagnols se passent fort bien du *ph* grec pour écrire *farmacia* ou *filosofia* et ils ne sont pas plus barbares que nous.

■■ What kinds of objection are these responses to?

■■ Do they strike you as adequate?

Many of the anti-reformers were distinctly left-of-centre figures. Danièle Mitterrand, for instance, and the members of the Comité Robespierre (founded to demand 'la guillotine morale du mépris contre les techno-crates sans âme et sans pensée qui ont osé profaner notre langue').

■■ Why, on the face of it, should this be surprising, and do there seem to be any reasons for it?

■■■ What is your own view of the desirability of reforming French spelling?

Combating sexism in language

Over the last dozen years, in Quebec, Belgium and Switzerland – and even for a time in France – government backing has been forthcoming for various proposals to counter the sex discrimination which many feel to be inherent in French grammar and vocabulary. Here are some indications of problem areas.

1   The following reply was given by *Le Figaro* – as long ago as 1948, admittedly – to a reader enquiring whether a female museum curator should be called a *conservateur* or a *conservatrice*:

> Il est flatteur pour une femme d'avoir un titre masculin, et par conséquent on devrait dire non seulement Madame le Conservateur, mais Madame le Conseiller, Madame l'Inspecteur.
>
> (quoted in Georgin 1957: 48)

2   Many people's first reaction to the following is that it's contradictory:

> Blessé dans un accident de voiture où il vient de perdre son père, un enfant doit subir une intervention chirurgicale. Aux urgences, le chirurgien déclare qu'il ne peut pas l'opérer puisque c'est son fils.

3   The following is perfectly correct in terms of the standard rules of agreement and pronoun use:

> 2 hommes et 99 femmes se sont réunis. Ils ont décidé de protester . . .

4   Traditionally the following masculine and feminine pairs are found in standard French: *un serveur/une serveuse*; *un employé/une employée*; *un ouvrier/une ouvrière*. But not: *un sénateur/une sénatrice*; *un chirurgien/une chirurgienne*; *un député/une députée*. And whereas the boss's female secretary is <u>une</u> *secrétaire*, a female foreign minister would be *Madame <u>le</u> secrétaire d'Etat aux affaires étrangères*. And the managing director remains <u>le</u> *directeur-général*, even when on maternity leave!

■   What do (1) and (2) suggest about attitudes towards professional women?

■■   What incongruities of language are invoked in (3)?

■■   What do the examples in (4) suggest about the relative status of men and women in French society? Think of some more cases like these.

In 1984 a *Commission de féminisation des noms de métiers* was set up by Yvette Roudy, then Minister for Women's Rights in the French Socialist government, in an attempt to combat this sort of bias. Most of the recommendations were adopted by Parliament two years later and embodied in a Ministry circular, though it has to be said that they have not been very closely heeded. What is more, they incurred the wrath of the Académie française. In Quebec, the Office de la langue française has produced its own series of proposals, which have had a much more noticeable effect on usage in Canada. Quite successful too have been the official recommendations made in 1994 by the Communauté française de Belgique, and in 1991 by the Swiss compilers of the *Dictionnaire féminin–masculin des professions*. (This was published with the backing of the cantonal governments in Geneva and Jura, and lists recommended feminine forms for the names of around 4,000 professions and trades.)

The kinds of innovation proposed in France were based on traditional patterns (but feminine endings such as *-esse* were avoided since they often have derogatory overtones: *doctoresse*, etc.). Thus:

1 *un/une élève* (difference indicated only by the article)
2 *un noyé/une noyée* (m and f nouns differ in spelling only)
3 *un châtelain/une châtelaine* (m and f nouns differ in pronunciation as well as in spelling)
4 *un acteur/une actrice*
   un mineur/une mineure } (various patterns for *-eur*)
   un serveur/une serveuse

The feminines recommended for the following masculines come under the categories indicated:

le député	2
le notaire	1
le chef	1
le maire	1
l'inspecteur	4
l'écrivain	3

■ Work out the recommended forms.

Specific proposals varied somewhat from one francophone country to another. On the whole the recommendations from France were the most conventional, with a strong preference for category 1.

■■ What do you think of the following proposals (variously from Belgium, Canada and Switzerland)?

auteure; cheffe; consulesse; prud'femme; sapeuse-pompière.

A *conseil des prud'hommes* is the equivalent of an industrial tribunal, so a female member of one would be a *prud'femme*, in Switzerland at least.

Not only names of trades and professions have received attention, as is shown by the following excerpt from the Introduction to the *Dictionnaire féminin–masculin*:

> Il reste à celles et à ceux qui sont convaincu-e-s de l'égalité des droits à s'emparer de ces mots, à les faire leurs . . . N'oublions jamais que le français appartient à toutes les femmes, à tous les hommes de la francophonie et non à une élite d'expert-e-s. C'est à chacun et à chacune d'entre nous qu'il appartient désormais d'user de ces mots nouveaux.

- ■ What features of 'gender-neutral language' can you spot here?

- ■■ How do these changes in French usage compare with those that are becoming more and more common in anglophone countries? Consider, for example, the use of terms like *firefighter*, *chair(person)*, *s/he* (or *they*).

- ■■■ Does the relative absence of grammatical gender in English make it inherently less biased than French and hence more amenable to change?

In France, the proposals gave rise to a lively debate. The essence of the pro-reformers' point of view was that distinctive feminine forms give women a clear social and professional identity. It makes them 'visible', so to speak. By contrast, the official view of the Académie française was that masculines are 'unmarked' forms which can be used of either sex (just as *chien* can refer to any dog unless it is important to specify that it's female). Since recent 'unofficial' feminines like *cheffesse*, *doctoresse* or *poétesse* have tended to take on derogatory associations, the best solution, according to the Academy, is to continue to use the 'unmarked masculine' in all cases where no separate feminine exists traditionally.

- ■■ In what respects is the reformers' view the opposite of the Academy's?

- ■■ Which do you find more valid?

- ■■ Does the Academy's view help in respect of any of the problem areas on pp. 193–4?

Some of the most distinguished citizens of France are buried in the Panthéon in Paris, on the façade of which is engraved the following inscription:

AUX GRANDS HOMMES LA PATRIE RECONNAISSANTE

In 1995 the transfer to the Panthéon of the remains of the physicist Marie Curie triggered off a predictable argument.

- What was the problem?

■■ State the point of view of an Academician and someone opposed to sexism in language.

■■■ What solutions can you envisage?

And much irritation was caused among those favouring *féminisation* by press comments like the following which appeared, somewhat surprisingly, in *Le Monde*:

> Lutter contre le sexisme des mots, donner aux femmes écrivains le statut d'écrivaines, aux députés du beau sexe le beau nom de députées et aux femmes ministres leurs portefeuilles de ministresses, tel est le projet qu'assigne Madame Y. Roudy à une commission qu'elle vient de mettre en place.
>
> La première femme qui sera élue cheftaine de l'Etat aura ainsi devant elle une septennate pour tenir, avec la gouvernemente, les engageaisons de sa programmature électorale et conduire la France sur les chemines de la progresserie dont elle a tant besoigne.
>
> (B. Frappat, *Le Monde*, 28 April 1984)

- Identify words invented for satirical purposes by this writer.

■■ Say whether you agree with the reformers' claim that such comments are irresponsible and distort the work of the Commission.

■■■ Conduct a survey of job advertisements in the French-language press, in order to establish what effect, if any, the recommendations about feminization have had in practice.

A further problem, and one that is probably even less easy to deal with, concerns the differing meanings or associations of corresponding male and female terms.

■■ Can you comment on the difference between:

- *un maître; une maîtresse*
- *un courtisan; une courtisane*
- *un coureur; une coureuse*
- *un couturier; une couturière*
- *un homme public; une femme publique*
- *un gars; une garce*

Even terms as basic as *homme* and *femme* are not simply mirror images of one another. Under the definitions of *homme* in *Le Petit Robert* are to be found predominantly positive examples of usage such as:

> *parole d'homme; bel homme; brave homme; homme de génie; homme de goût,*

whereas the examples under *femme* include a number of 'negatively polarized' phrases like:

> *grosse femme mal faite; femme de mauvaise vie; femme inconstante; raisonnement de femme soûle* (i.e. «raisonnement illogique»).

■■ The claim is sometimes made that sexism (conscious or unconscious) is widespread among dictionary-makers. Find further examples in the *Petit Robert* and other dictionaries, and try to establish whether this claim can be justified.

Official neologisms

Since the appearance in 1964 of Étiemble's celebrated *Parlez-vous franglais?*, there has been widespread unease about the number of Anglo-American words and expressions entering French usage. In a bid to stem the tide at least to some extent, governments, both in Europe and in North America, have been making determined attempts to launch French terms for a variety of new devices, processes and concepts. The new terms are known as *néologismes*, and the business of inventing them is sometimes called *la néologie*. Usually the aim is to provide alternatives to English terms already or potentially in common use in French, though there are a few official neologisms which don't have any obvious English 'rivals': for example *sidéen* ('malade atteint du sida').

Had this sort of official concern existed in the 1830s, then French railway terminology (partly derived from English) might have looked somewhat different today, with *ornière de fer* instead of *rail*, *galerie* (*souterraine*) instead of *tunnel*, and *allège* instead of *tender*. All these alternatives were in use in the earliest 'days of steam', but, sadly perhaps, were destined to disappear (Wexler 1950).

Dictionary entries reflect the work of the terminologists. For instance, under BULLDOZER (stated to be a *mot américain*), the *Petit Larousse Illustré* states that *bouteur* is an official alternative. Similarly *baladeur* is given for WALKMAN.

■   Use the *PLI* to find out the 'anglicismes déconseillés' for which the following are the official recommendations:

   auto-caravane; *cadreur*; *remue-méninges*; *transbordeur*.

The French terms recommended in such dictionary entries have been devised by *commissions de terminologie* (twenty or so in number) attached to various government ministries. Commission members include technical specialists, journalists and lexicographers, and, increasingly, the work done in France is carried out in consultation with equivalent bodies in Quebec, Belgium, Switzerland and other francophone countries. Proposals are co-ordinated by the Délégation générale à la langue française, approved by act of Parliament and published in the *Journal Officiel* (the record of Parliamentary proceedings). Every few years official dictionaries of new terms appear: the following is a typical entry from the *Dictionnaire des termes officiels de la langue française* of 1994:

PLACEMENT DES PIEDS

   n.m. *Domaine*: Sport/Golf. *Définition*: Positionnement des pieds du joueur devant la balle. *Anglais*: stance. *Source*: Arrêté du sport du 11 décembre 1992. *J.O.* du 20 janvier 1993.

■   What information is contained in such a dictionary entry?

In the next chapter the legislation accompanying the new coinages will be considered. For the time being, let's concentrate on the linguistic processes that are involved. Here are some further examples of official coinages from various Ministry commissions.

Défense
amerrissage forcé   ditching
missile de croisière   cruise missile
résistance à l'écrasement   crashworthiness
suraccélération   jerk
système autoentretien   bootstrap system

Economie et finances
bazarette   convenience store
capitaux fébriles   hot money
valeur de premier ordre   blue chip

Informatique
bogue   bug (in program)
doc (disque optique compact)   CD-ROM
ludiciel   game software
puce   chip
tel écran tel écrit   WYSIWYG

Ingénierie Nucléaire
rétrodiffusion   back scattering

Sciences et techniques spatiales
entrée d'air auxiliaire   blow-in door
télécommande   remote control

Techniques de la communication
haut-parleur de graves *or* boumeur   boomer
haut-parleur d'aigus *or* tuiteur   tweeter
heures de grande écoute   prime time

Télédetection aérospatiale
scanneur   scanner

Tourisme et loisirs
ciné-parc   drive-in cinema
restauration rapide   fast food
voyagiste   tour operator

Transports

billetterie	ticketing
conteneur	container
ferroutage	piggy-back

From the Office de la langue française, Quebec

animalerie	pet-shop
dépanneur	convenience store
éditique	desk-top publishing
grand déjeuner	brunch
jardinerie	garden centre

From the Journal Officiel du Sénégal

Primature	Prime Minister's office

In almost all these examples, the neologism is intended either to replace an English term already in use, or to forestall the introduction into French of a term current in Anglo-American usage. The French term:

–   may be virtually the same in form as the corresponding English term
–   may result from the adaptation of an English term to French spelling and/or pronunciation
–   may be the literal translation of an English word or expression
–   may involve substituting an abstract French expression for a concrete one in English (or vice versa)
–   may involve a change of one or more parts of speech as between the English and French equivalents
–   may involve an image being altered or eliminated
–   may amount to an explanation or paraphrase of an English term
–   may be an independent creation with no direct formal relationship to its English equivalent.

■   Say which of these categories corresponds to each of the neologisms given so far, and indicate any other modes of word formation that strike you.

■■   Do any of these official neologisms seem to you particularly praise-worthy or particularly inept?

The author of an article entitled 'Les irréductibles du vocabulaire audio-visuel' (*Libération* 18 February 1983) had the following comments to make about certain recalcitrant items which more or less defeated the terminology experts (the three cases quoted here all come from the fields of film-making and advertising):

FLASH: Ouf, on n'achève pas les vieux chevaux. *Flash* est intégré dans le patrimoine linguistique français depuis 1918. Il a donc été décidé de ne pas y toucher.

RUSH: *Épreuve* a été proposé, mais a essuyé un tollé général de la profession puisque le terme anglais contient l'idée de rapidité qui est absent de son équivalent français. Aucune autre autre solution n'a pu voir le jour.

SPOT: On a eu beau se dépenser dans tous les sens, aucun équivalent n'a pu lui être trouvé. L'arrêté de 1972 prétendait imposer «message publicitaire» mais faisait là l'économie de ce qui caractérise ce type de message, sa brièveté. Que l'on se rassure donc, le spot a encore une longue vie devant lui.

■■ What problems face the terminologists in cases like these?

■■ To date, some 5,000 neologisms have been devised. Do you think this is sufficient to meet the need?

■■ What is your own view of the usefulness and desirability of terminology commissions?

The work of the commissions still continues, though output is not as great as it used to be. Nor are the media debates about the desirability and effectiveness of *néologie* as lively as they were in the early years. Moreover, devising new terminology is one thing, but getting the general public to use it is quite another. A survey of language use carried out in 1994 among forty respondents from a range of social backgrounds asked the following question (Le Maitre 1994):

Lequel des mots suivants utilisez-vous le plus volontiers?
    baladeur ou *walkman*
    logiciel ou *software*
    cadreur ou *cameraman*

affiche ou *poster*
[etc. . . .]

and obtained results like the following:

baladeur 11	walkman 27	les deux 1	sans opinion 1
logiciel 34	software 1	les deux 1	sans opinion 4
cadreur 2	cameraman 33	les deux 1	sans opinion 4
affiche 6	poster 30	les deux 3	sans opinion 1

■■ Comment on these figures. What do they suggest about the accept-
ability of official neologisms, and what do you think would be the
general reaction to other examples – those given on pp. 200–1, for
instance?

■■■ Conduct your own surveys among francophones, getting reactions
about spelling reform, the 'feminization of the language' and new,
government-inspired terminology.

■■■ Is successful State intervention possible and desirable in matters of
language?

Further reading

Chapters 1, 6 and 7 of Sanders (1993) provide information about terminology commissions, language feminization and orthography respectively.
Offord (forthcoming) reproduces official texts setting out the details of the
spelling reform and the Roudy feminization proposals. *Le Livre de
l'orthographe* (Pivot 1989) deals with a range of aspects of spelling and
spelling reform. Goosse (1991) is an account of the reform by a member
of the commission responsible for devising it. For an extended application
of the principles of gender-neutral language, see the *Dictionnaire
féminin–masculin des professions* (1991).

• • •

Chapter 12

Defending and preserving the language

A language in decline?

As we saw in Chapter 4, it has long been the aim of governments to provide France with a single standardized national language – specifically the variety of French elaborated ('perfected', it was generally believed) by the grammarians of the seventeenth and eighteenth centuries, and originally used largely by the aristocracy in Paris and Versailles.

Such an aim gave rise to anxiety that this prestige form of French might be 'contaminated' by provincial usage and by the speech-habits of the lower orders. The conviction grew that the norms of the standard language needed to be 'defended', and rules of 'correct usage' unambiguously laid down for the uninitiated. This was the point of departure for the tradition of *défense de la langue*, a tradition that is as robust today as it was in the years immediately following the Revolution.

The most extreme protagonists of this 'normative' or 'prescriptivist' tradition (often called 'purists' by others, though they are reluctant to apply the term to themselves) tend to see innovation and departure from the norm as potentially threatening, and therefore to be resisted. Here is a typical expression of this kind of view, taken from a French Academy-sponsored journal, the mission of which is clear from its title:

> Notre langue est de plus en plus menacée, tant dans sa forme, par la prolifération des fautes de style, de grammaire, d'orthographe, que par l'invasion de la langue anglaise.
>
> (*Défense de la langue française* March 1991)

This chapter will provide material on the Academy itself, and on the two problems referred to in this quotation: anglicisms, and general 'sloppiness' of usage.

The French Academy

The tradition of State involvement in regulating the language goes back to the founding of the Académie française in 1634 – a time when, even among the educated few, much uncertainty existed about matters of usage. (Should *période* be masculine or feminine? Should one say *prie-on* or *prie-t-on*? etc.) The new institution, set up with royal backing, was given the task of producing a definitive grammar and dictionary of the language: its aims were forcefully – if unofficially – expressed as follows by one of its founding members:

> ... nettoyer la langue des ordures qu'elle avait contractées, ou dans la bouche du peuple, ou dans la foule de Paris, ou par les mauvais usages des courtisans ignorants ...
>
> (Faret, quoted in Brunot 1909: 34)

■■ What assumptions about language and its users underlie a (typically purist) statement like this?

The *Grammar* did not in fact appear until three centuries had elapsed. When it was eventually published, in 1932, it turned out to be a feeble affair, was instantly subjected to a barrage of hostile criticism, and subsequently disowned by the Academy itself. The *Dictionary* had a somewhat better fate, and the first edition came out in 1694, despite numerous defects that were much criticized at the time (entries weren't in alphabetical order, and even the word *académie* was nearly left out by mistake!). In fact, better and wider-ranging dictionaries were already being published by private individuals, for example by Antoine Furetière, the compiler of the *Dictionnaire Universel* of 1690, and himself a former Academician. To him we owe the following, no doubt somewhat prejudiced, description of the seventeenth-century Academy's proceedings:

> ... cela se fait avec tant de bruit et de confusion, que les plus sages se taisent, et que l'avis des plus violents l'emporte. Celui qui crie le plus haut, c'est celui qui a raison ... Quand un Bureau est composé de cinq ou six personnes, il y en a un qui lit, un qui opine, deux qui causent, un qui dort et un qui s'amuse à lire quelque Dictionnaire qui est sur la table.
>
> (Furetière, quoted in Brunot 1911: 37)

The Academy still meets once a week in the Institut de France, on the quai de Conti opposite the Louvre, with the assistance of full-time professional lexicographers and, one presumes, in a more serious atmosphere than in the seventeenth century. It is currently publishing, volume by volume, the ninth edition of the *Dictionary*, work on which began in 1936. Completion is anticipated around 2001. Quite a stir was created in the mid-1990s when it emerged that words as fashionable as *drugstore* and as colloquial as *emmerdeur* were being included.

Here is some further information about the current *Dictionary*.

> *Dictionnaire de l'Académie française.* 5 volumes, 50,000 entries (projected), no illustrations, no proper names. Price approximately 150F per volume (paperback), 480F (hardback).

And here are details of two categories of 'rival' dictionaries:

1   *Le Nouveau Petit Robert* (1994 edition). 1 volume, 59,000 entries, no illustrations. A second volume contains 36,000 proper names, this time *with* illustrations. Price 379F (volume 2, 389F).

     Le Petit Larousse Illustré (1995 edition). 1 volume, 58,900 entries (plus 25,500 proper names in same volume). Illustrations throughout. Price 245F.

2   *Le Grand Robert de la langue française.* 9 volumes, 100,000 entries. No proper names or illustrations. Price approx 500F per volume.

     Le Grand Larousse. 6 volumes, 100,000 entries. No proper names. Price approx 480F per volume.

     Le Trésor de la langue française. 16 volumes, 100,000 entries. No proper names or illustrations. Published by the state-funded Centre national de la recherche scientifique. Records usage up to 1960 only. Price approx 700F per volume.

The dictionaries in Group 1 are relatively concise desk-top works of reference; those in Group 2 obviously contain far more detail and are most typically found in libraries.

■   With which of the two categories has the *Dictionnaire de l'Académie* the closest affinity?

■ Use the above information, and the dictionaries themselves if available, as a basis for comparing the Academy Dictionary with its 'rivals'. Also, compare some entries in as many of the dictionaries as possible.

■■ How does the range of information it provides measure up to that provided by other dictionaries in either category? Take account of such features as pronunciation, etymology (word history), quotations (genuine or invented), etc.

■■ Can you rate the Academy Dictionary in terms of 'value for money'?

Apart from compiling the Dictionary, the Academy issues periodic *mises en garde* about points of grammar and vocabulary (of the kind illustrated on p. 217), and is consulted about new official terminology and about spelling-reform projects. To be one of the Academicians (*les quarante Immortels*) remains among the greatest honours the Republic can bestow.

■■ All the current Academicians are listed in *Quid* (in the section on 'Les Lettres'). Using the information given there and, if desired, taking further biographical details from *Who's Who in France*, make an analysis of the membership of the Academy in terms of age, sex, occupational background, social standing and likely suitability for dictionary-making.

■■■ Though the Academy is often referred to as 'la gardienne de la langue', its role today is largely symbolic and ceremonial. Why do you think this is?

Anglicisms and the loi Toubon of 1994

Already in 1975 an unsuccessful attempt had been made to legislate against anglicisms and to encourage the use of official neologisms. In 1994 Jacques Toubon, then *ministre de la culture et de la francophonie*, undertook to revive this earlier legislation and to extend its provisions. The basic details of the 'loi relative à l'emploi de la langue française' are given in the following summary:

On pourra continuer à se promener dans la rue en *blue-jean* et *sweat-shirt* avec un walkman sur les oreilles sans risquer l'amende ou la prison. Le nouveau projet de loi . . . se veut plus utilitaire, destiné aux consommateurs, aux salariés et au public, qu'idéologique.

Trouvant ses racines dans l'ordonnance de Villers-Cotterêts de 1539 . . . dans la Constitution (la langue de la République est le français) et, plus récemment, dans une loi du 31 décembre 1975, le projet du ministre ordonne que contrats, offres d'emploi et documents internes à une entreprise soient rédigés dans la langue de Molière, tout comme les inscriptions destinées au public (du style «sortie de secours»), ou les modes d'emploi accompagnant des objets. Le français doit régner dans l'enseignement ainsi que dans les émissions et les messages publicitaires des radios et des télévisions.

Quant aux participants francophones des congrès et des colloques, ils auront la possibilité d'utiliser leur langue, et disposeront d'un programme des manifestations ainsi que d'un résumé des débats en français.

(*Lire*, April 1994: 8)

■■ How does the law guarantee the individual linguistic freedoms referred to in the first paragraph?

■■■ In what ways do you think the internationalisation of the business, media and academic worlds has created a need for the various provisions listed here?

At no point in the bill are any languages other than French specifically mentioned. It may seem self-evident that English is implicitly referred to throughout, but supporters of regional languages were very alarmed by the proposals (though eventually placated).

■■ Why should this have been the case?

The following press articles describe the progression of the bill through the National Assembly and the Senate during the spring and summer of 1994. The well-attended and widely reported debates in the French Parliament reflect the broader national discussion, even though fewer passions were aroused than by the spelling controversy. The middle-of-the-road view seems to have been that the law, although a worthy initiative and deserving of support, was in practice unenforceable. However, more vigorous positions were taken up on both sides.

First reading: excerpts from the debate in the Senate, April 1994
(C. Blandin, *Le Monde*, 14 and 15 April 1994)

Les plus virulents des sénateurs ont entrepris une chasse aux sorcières contre «*l'anglo-américain*», en criant haro sur la radio, la télévision et la publicité, responsables de la «*gangrène*» du français par les termes étrangers. Pour lutter contre cette évolution, une seule solution: «*La réaction sécuritaire s'impose*», a affirmé Marc Auriol (RPR). «*Il est grand temps de renforcer la loi de 1975 par un texte plus approfondi et prévoyant un dispositif répressif*», a renchéri Philippe Richert (UC).

Françoise Seligmann (PS) a pris le contre-pied de cette position en se déclarant choquée par la «*résonance quelque peu xénophobe du texte. Vous voulez édifier une sorte de ligne Maginot de la langue derrière laquelle le français serait à l'abri des intrusions étrangères . . . Nous ne sommes plus à l'époque des pays hermétiquement fermés sur eux-mêmes*», a-t-elle lancé à l'adresse du ministre, qu'elle a mis en garde contre son choix de «*recourir à la contrainte pour prohiber des expressions et des termes étrangers. Votre méthode risque de creuser encore davantage le fossé qui vous sépare de la jeunesse*, a-t-elle souligné, *car vos interdits frapperaient en premier lieu les émissions de radio et de télévision et les messages publicitaires destinés aux jeunes*».

Quant à Yvan Renar (PC), il s'est demandé si le gouvernement ne faisait pas fausse route en s'attachant plus aux effets de la régression du français qu'à ses causes: «*On n'imposera pas le français comme langue d'usage scientifique par décret. Il faut avant tout créer une recherche suffisamment forte pour que le français ait droit de cité dans les publications et banques de données scientifiques*» . . .

Et le combat cessa . . . sous les cris de «*Vive la République! Vive la France*» de Maurice Schumann (RPR). Il était 13 heures. Ironique, Emmanuel Hamel (RPR) souligna toute l'importance du texte en discussion: ce mercredi, le restaurant du Sénat proposait à ses convives un . . . «*mixed grill*».

- Why is Emmanuel Hamel's comment described as 'ironic'?

- ■ To what extent did the representatives of Left, Right and Centre express views that fit their political affiliations?

Second reading: excerpts from the debate in the Assembly, May 1994
(C. Blandin, *Le Monde*, 5 May 1994)

Adepte de la géopolitique, M. Toubon a pris de la hauteur pour brosser un préoccupant état du monde. «*Depuis la chute du mur de Berlin, l'ordre ancien n'existe plus*, a-t-il rappelé, *et nous voyons apparaître un seul modèle culturel, politique, économique, inspiré de l'économie de marché, avec ses bienfaits, mais, aussi, avec ses tares. Ce n'est pas parce que le monde est un qu'il doit être uniforme*», a-t-il ajouté . . . Au reste, ce texte est porteur d'un message universel . . . «*Préserver le français, langue de la liberté, de l'égalité et de la démocratie, est un enjeu pour tous les peuples épris de nos valeurs*», a-t-il assuré . . .

Pierre Lellouche (RPR) a bien voulu reconnaître au texte le «*mérite de marquer un coup d'arrêt à la dégradation de notre langue*», mais il «*s'interroge*». «*Le problème est-il vraiment celui d'une menace de l'extérieur*? a-t-il questionné. *Si colonisation culturelle il y a, n'est-elle pas, avant tout, dans nos têtes? L'usage dicte ici sa loi et non l'inverse*», a-t-il lancé à l'adresse de ceux qui auraient oublié que «*la langue ne se décrète pas*».

Laurent Dominati (UDF), lui, ne s'interroge plus, car il s'inquiète déjà. Il se dit préoccupé de l'image renvoyée à l'étranger par ce débat franco-français: «*Je crains que cette loi, qui cherche à préserver la langue française assaillie par l'anglais, ne montre au monde entier que le français est devenu une langue assiégée, minoritaire, une langue du passé . . . Faut-il dire aux étudiants du monde entier que la langue française est une langue dont l'usage, en France, a besoin d'être imposé par l'Etat sous peine d'amende*?» En bon libéral, M. Dominati n'accepte pas de voir la puissance publique s'ériger en «*police des mots. Je plaide pour l'indépendance de la langue française, non seulement face à l'anglais, mais aussi et surtout vis-à-vis de l'Etat*», a-t-il dit. M. Toubon a pris un air renfrogné en écoutant cet éloge du libéralisme linguistique.

Didier Mathus (PS) a été plus sévère encore pour dénoncer une loi répressive. «*L'image de la langue française doit-elle être associée à celle d'un gendarme armé d'un gros bâton? Votre texte est une sorte de loi sécuritaire*, a-t-il regretté. *On y décèle la tentation d'expulser les mots étrangers comme on expulse les étrangers en situation irrégulière . . . Allez-vous installer des douaniers du langage et des inspecteurs du vocabulaire?*» Bien entendu, M Toubon n'était pas d'accord, lui qui ne souhaite «*qu'interdire qu'on interdise l'usage du français*».

- How similar are the views of P. Lellouche and L. Dominati?

■■ At the end of the third paragraph, what does the reporter understand by 'libéralisme linguistique'? What parallels are there between this and political or economic liberalism?

■■ How sensible do you find the comments made by D. Mathus?

■■ Despite what is stated in the earlier excerpt from *Lire*, the bill seems not to have been motivated solely by 'utilitarian' considerations (i.e. about the comprehensibility of contracts, signs and instructions on appliances), but to have had quite a strong 'ideological' basis. What aspects of this are revealed in J. Toubon's remarks to the Assembly?

The Socialist deputies abstained in the voting, and subsequently fifty-five of them appealed to the Conseil Constitutionnel on the grounds that certain articles of the law were unconstitutional.

Dans le collimateur, neuf articles du texte . . . interdisant notamment l'emploi d'un terme étranger dans toute description d'un bien ou dans tout affichage public. *«De telles dispositions portent manifeste-ment atteinte à la fois à la liberté de communication, proclamée par l'article 11 de la Déclaration des droits de l'homme . . . et à la liberté du commerce et de l'industrie»*, expliquent les députés.

Certes, conviennent-ils, de telles libertés peuvent être limitées s'il y a trouble à l'ordre public ou menace envers des libertés de rang équivalent. Mais . . . «on ne voit pas quelle liberté constitutionnelle-ment protégée souffre lorsqu'un Français décide de s'exprimer en une autre langue que la sienne».

(*Libération*, 6 July 1994)

- On what grounds did the deputies claim the law to be unconstitutional?

The essence of the Council's ruling was reported as follows by *Le Monde*:

Le Conseil Constitutionnel . . . a censuré partiellement la loi de Jacques Toubon . . . Au nom de la «libre communication des pensées et . . . des opinions», proclamée par la Déclaration des droits de l'homme de 1789, il a refusé à l'Etat le droit d'imposer, à des person-nes privées, l'usage d'un français qu'il codifierait lui-même . . . L'Etat aura tout de même la possibilité d'imposer l'utilisation de la langue

> telle qu'il l'aura codifiée aux personnes morales de droit public et aux
> personnes privées dans l'accomplissement d'un service public.
>
> (T. Bréhier, *Le Monde*, 30 July 1994)

un français qu'il codifierait lui-même: this refers to the official terms issued by
Ministry commissions (see Chapter 11); *personne morale de droit public*: bodies
such as government departments, local councils, State-run schools.

In practice, as the Paris correspondent of the *Observer* pointed out (31
July 1994), this means, for example, that the neologism *coussin gonflable*
must be used by French transport officials, while car salesmen can still talk
about *un airbag*. Similarly, a tourist office will put on a *bande video
promotionnelle*, while a travel agent can offer potential customers *un clip*.

■ How has the Constitutional Council's ruling had these effects?

■ The name *'Booster'* was given to one of their new games by the
publicly owned Société française des jeux. Why was this deemed,
in the newsletter of the Délégation général à la langue française, to
be an infringement of the law?

■■ How successful do you think the loi Toubon is likely to prove in the
attempt to stem the incursion of anglicisms?

■■■ In what way is there a conflict here between two legacies of 1789:
the Declaration of the Rights of Man on the one hand, and the
French Republic on the other (the language of which was, in a 1992
amendment to the Constitution, declared to be French)?

The presence on the statute-book of the loi Toubon, and continued
violations of the law like the ones just referred to, have revived the
tradition of associations pledged to defend the interests of language users.
Currently, several of these are grouped together as the 'Association Droit
de comprendre' (DDC), and at the end of 1995 initiated a successful
prosecution of The Body Shop for failing to provide French translations
of the instructions and warnings accompanying its cosmetic products. The
president of the association, in a letter to the Finance Ministry, justified
the prosecution on the grounds that The Body Shop were misinforming
their non-anglophone customers in a potentially dangerous way. He also
drew attention to their much publicized links with the environmental
movement and to their anti-nuclear stance, accusing them of seeking
unfair commercial advantage over the French cosmetics industry. (At the

time, a series of French nuclear tests was the object of worldwide condemnation.)

■■ How is it that the legislation still permits such a ruling, despite the decision of the Constitutional Council?

■■ What links between linguistic, commercial and political considerations are implicit in the remarks made by the president of DDC?

■■ Do you sympathize or not with the stand taken by DDC?

The prescriptivist tradition

The 'internal weaknesses' that cause alarm essentially involve aspects of grammar and vocabulary where formal and informal registers have diverged, the colloquial variants being disapproved of and the literary ones recommended. The more prescriptive the commentator, the less likely he or she will be to distinguish between situations where colloquial forms are appropriate and those where they are not (see Chapter 9). Here are some of the most frequently criticized 'mistakes' (the time-honoured two-column layout of the concise grammar guide is reproduced here):

NE DITES PAS . . .	MAIS DITES . . .
*un milliard de francs est une somme d'argent conséquente	
après qu'il soit parti	
je préfère l'autre alternative	
solutionner un problème	
*sans qu'ils ne le sachent	
*je ne m'en rappelle pas	
aller au coiffeur	
commémorer un anniversaire.	

■ Using standard reference works if necessary, find out what each *faute de français* involves, and enter the 'correct' form in the 'Dites' column.

■ 'Errors' indicated by asterisks have been the object of condemnation since as long ago as the end of the eighteenth century, but still continue to be made. What does this suggest about the influence of normative grammarians on the evolution of the language?

■■ Why have words like *mistake* or *error* been placed between inverted commas here, and why do non-prescriptive linguists prefer to speak of 'non-standard forms'?

Many deviations of this kind are natural (even logical) developments, which is why they occur so frequently. Thus there is a understandable parallelism between *aller au coiffeur* and *aller à la poste, aller au marché,* etc.

■■ Which of the other errors listed above can you explain? Does the explanation 'excuse' the error?

■■ Explain the view that 'today's mistake is tomorrow's standard form'.

Faute de français is an umbrella term covering all kinds of deviation from the norm. Here, with illustrative examples (non-standard form first), are some more specific categories often encountered in guides to correct usage.

BARBARISME: *pécunier* for *pécuniaire*; *réouvrir* for *rouvrir*; *aéropage* for *aréopage* ('distinguished gathering').

PLÉONASME: *ajouter en plus* for *ajouter*; *préparer d'avance* for *préparer*; *collaborer ensemble* for *collaborer*.

IMPROPRIÉTÉ: *décade* for *décennie*; *rivière* for *fleuve*; *romanesque* for *romantique*.

SOLÉCISME: *quoiqu'il est tard* instead of *quoiqu'il soit tard*; *c'est les meilleures voitures* instead of *ce sont les meilleures voitures*.

■■ On the basis of these examples, can you define the kind of error which each category relates to?

Purists often use less neutral terminology than this. All the following phrases have, at some time or other in recent years, been applied in handbooks of correct usage to errors like the ones just considered:

flagrante impropriété; pernicieuse sottise; grossière impropriété; faute inexpiable; horreur; monstre authentique; outrage à notre langue; anglicisme éhonté; énormité de langage; pléonasme haïssable; abominable faute; solécisme ignoble; néologisme outrancier.

■ What kinds of emotional reaction are conveyed by expressions like these?

Normative grammarians do, of course, quite often have a rational basis for their likes and dislikes. Explanations like the following are typical. These come from a popular mini-paperback entitled *Je connais mieux le français* (Rat 1978: 22, 27, 34, 46).

NE DITES PAS . . .   MAIS DITES . . .

Il y avaient neuf à dix élèves présents   *Il y avait neuf ou dix élèves présents*

On peut dire: ce livre coûte de neuf *à* dix francs (car il peut coûter neuf francs cinquante). Mais on ne saurait parler de neuf élèves et demi ou de neuf élèves trois quarts.

De sous terre   *De dessous terre*

Dès la fin du XVIIᵉ siècle, l'Académie française, suivant Vaugelas, a proscrit l'usage de *sous* et *sur* et conseillé celui de *dessous* et de *dessus* après *à*, *de* et *par*.

Pallier aux difficultés   *Pallier les difficultés*

Pallier est un verbe transitif qui veut un complément direct (latin *palliare* «couvrir d'un manteau»). C'est par confusion avec *remédier* «porter remède à» que certains, à tort, disent ou écrivent *pallier à*. On remédie à un mal, à une difficulté; mais on pallie un mal ou une difficulté.

Se baser sur . . .   *Se fonder sur . . .*

La *base* d'un édifice se trouvant au ras du sol, et ses *fondations* au-dessous, ce sont elles et non la base qui donnent à la construction sa solidité. Royer-Collard, il y a plus d'un siècle, comme certains de

217

ses confrères de l'Académie proposaient d'admettre *se baser* au Dictionnaire, s'écria: «S'il entre, je sors!»

The following are four examples of the categories into which such explanations tend to fall:

(a) The erroneous form is illogical.
(b) There is a clash with the 'real' meaning of the word.
(c) The approved form is justified by its historical origins (usually the way its ancestor was used in Latin).
(d) The erroneous form has been condemned in the past by a leading authority (who may or may not have given reasons).

■ Find the appropriate category (or categories) for each of the quotations just given.

■■ How convincing do you find the explanations?

The wide divergencies between formal and informal usage (see Chapter 9), combined with the prestige of the normative tradition, have given many francophones a feeling of 'linguistic insecurity' – of having an inadequate command of French. This emerges in the following answers to a question in a survey conducted by *Lire* in March 1989:

Et la grammaire française: la trouvez-vous très facile, assez facile, assez difficile ou très difficile?

Très facile: 2%
Assez facile: 24%
Assez difficile: 51%
Très difficile: 22%
Ne se prononcent pas: 1%

■■ How is it possible for three-quarters of the native speakers of a language to find its grammar 'difficult'?

A sense of insecurity emerges no less strikingly in the following remarks by Parisians from various social backgrounds:

– La langue de tous les jours c'est pas le vrai français?
– Ah non, non, c'est pas le vrai français . . . c'est tout à fait vulgarisé,

moi je trouve . . . c'est pas du tout le vrai français . . . c'est pas du tout celui qu'on apprend à l'école . . . c'est certain . . . moi je parle le français très mal . . . avec beaucoup d'argot . . . ah oui.
(38-year old café manageress)

– . . . «t'es allé là-bas?» . . . hein . . . bah ça se dit pas normalement . . . normalement c'est «es-tu allé là-bas?» . . . nous on fait une faute comme ça . . . parce qu'on est toujours pressé.
(27-year-old workman)

. . . l'imparfait du subjonctif . . . le passé simple . . . ce sont des temps qui sont d'une autre époque peut-être . . . mais qui sont . . . le vrai français . . . le bon français emploie ces temps-là.
(59-year-old secretary)

– Qu'est-ce que vous pensez de votre façon de parler le français?
– Oh, elle est sûrement très mauvaise [rires]
– Pourquoi?
– Ché pas . . . tous les Français parlent mal [rires], eh, c'est comme tout le monde . . . on parle toujours un français qui n'est pas très pur, hein.
– Vous croyez?
– Y a des fautes de français, oui, on fait des fautes.
(33-year-old doctor)

(Fischer 1988: 77–8, 80, 101, 167)

■■ What do you think of the second speaker's explanation for the poor quality of his French («on est toujours pressé»)?

■■ What do expressions like le français, le vrai français, un français pur or ce qu'on dit normalement apparently refer to for these speakers?

■■ How did they acquire their view of what is 'real French' and what is not?

■■■ To what extent do your francophone friends and acquaintances feel that the French language needs defending and that the Government should take a leading role in this?

■■■ In your view, are the grammar and vocabulary of French under threat? If so, how seriously and in what respects?

Further reading

See Lodge (1993) for the role of the Academy and the grammarians in standardizing the language. Also Chapter 1 of Sanders (1993). Capelovici (1994) is a good example of a popular (and prescriptively oriented) guide to correct usage, with a lively introduction. The anti-purist point of view is put across equally spiritedly by Leeman-Bouix (1994). Books lamenting the alleged decline of the language are numerous: the classic is Étiemble (1964); other examples are de Broglie (1986) and Léopardini (1994). The Toubon legislation is too recent for anything to have been published about it in book form, but Offord (forthcoming) reproduces the official text, and Saint-Robert (1986) gives the inside story of the similar attempt made in the mid-1970s to discourage the use of foreign words.

• • •

Bibliography

Abou, S. and Haddad, K. (eds) (1994) *Une Francophonie différentielle*, Paris: L'Harmattan.

Ager, D. (1995) *'Francophonie' in the 1990s: Problems and Opportunities*, Clevedon: Multilingual Matters.

Alexandre, R. (1991) *Notre Entreprise est formidable*, Paris: Payot.

Arends, J., Muysken, P. and Smith, N. (eds) (1995) *Pidgins and Creoles*, Amsterdam: Benjamins.

Arnold, M. (1968) *Petites conversations*, London: Hulton Educational Publications.

Asher, R.E. and Simpson, J.M.Y. (eds) (1994) *The Encyclopedia of Language and Linguistics*, Oxford: Pergamon.

Baker, P. (1972) *Kreol: A Description of Mauritian Creole*, London: Hurst.

Batchelor, R.E. and Offord, M.H. (1982) *A Guide to Contemporary French Usage*, Cambridge: Cambridge University Press.

Bauche, H. (1928) *Le Langage populaire: grammaire, syntaxe et dictionnaire du français tel qu'on le parle dans le peuple, avec tous les termes d'argot usuels* (2nd edn.), Paris: Payot.

Bentahila, A. (1983) *Language Attitudes among Arabic–French Bilinguals in Morocco*, Clevedon: Multilingual Matters.

Bernard, P. (1993) *L'Immigration*, Paris: Le Monde Editions.

Bernet, C. and Rézeau, P. (1989) *Dictionnaire du français parlé: le monde des expressions familières*, Paris: Seuil.

Blanchet, P. (1994) 'Problèmes méthodologiques de l'évaluation des pratiques sociolinguistiques en langues "régionales" ou "minoritaires"', *Langage et Société* 69: 93–106.

Boissel, P. (1991) 'Peut-on dire qu'une pratique dialectale est terminée dans un milieu donné?', in J.-C. Bouvier and C. Martel (eds) *Les Français et leurs langues*, Aix-en-Provence: Publications de l'Université de Provence.

Bouvier, J.-C. and Martel, C. (eds) (1991) *Les Français et leurs langues*, Aix-en-Provence: Publications de l'Université de Provence.

Bovet, L. (1988) 'Le français en Suisse Romande', *Présence francophone* 29: 7–26.

Bright, W. (ed.) (1992) *International Encyclopedia of Linguistics*, New York: Oxford University Press.

de Broglie, G. (1986) *Le Français pour qu'il vive*, Paris: Gallimard.

Bruno, G. (1877) *Le Tour de France par deux enfants, devoir et patrie, livre de lecture courante*, Paris: Belin.

Brunot, F. (1909) *Histoire de la langue française des origines à 1900*, vol. III, 1, Paris: Colin.

—— (1911) *Histoire de la langue française des origines à 1900*, vol. IV, 1, Paris: Colin.

Capelovici, J. (1994) *Guide du français correct: répertoire des difficultés de la langue écrite et parlée*, Paris: Le Livre de poche.

Caradec, F. (1989) *N'ayons pas peur des mots: dictionnaire du français argotique et populaire*, Paris: Larousse.

Carton, F. (1981) 'Les parlers ruraux de la région Nord-Picardie: situation sociolinguistique', *International Journal of the Sociology of Language* 29: 15–28.

—— (1983) *Les Accents des Français*, Paris: Hachette.

—— (1987) 'Les accents régionaux', in G. Vermes and J. Boutet (eds) *France, pays multilingue*, Paris: L'Harmattan.

Cavanna, F. (1978) *Les Ritals*, Paris: Belfond.

Chaudenson, R. (1979) *Les Créoles français*, Paris: Nathan.

—— (1991) *La Francophonie: représentations, réalités, perspectives*, Paris: Didier.

—— (1995) *Les Créoles*, Paris: Presses Universitaires de France.

Commission of the European Communities (1986), *Linguistic Minorities in Countries Belonging to the European Community*, Luxembourg: Office for Official Publications of the European Communities.

Comrie, B. (1987) *The World's Major Languages*, London: Croom-Helm.

CREDIF (1969) *Enquête sur le langage de l'enfant français, Document 2*, Paris: Centre de recherche et d'étude pour la diffusion du français.

Crystal, D. (1987) *The Cambridge Encyclopedia of Language*, Cambridge: Cambridge University Press.

—— (1992) *An Encyclopedic Dictionary of Language and Languages*, Oxford: Blackwell.

Cuq, J.-P. (1991) *Le Français langue seconde: origines d'une notion et implications didactiques*, Paris: Hachette.

Dabène, L. (1990) 'Le parler bilingue issus [sic] de l'immigration en France', in R. Jacobson (ed.) *Codeswitching as a Worldwide Phenomenon*, New York: Peter Lang.

Dabène, L. and Billiez, J. (1987) 'Les parlers des jeunes issus de l'immigration', in G. Vermes and J. Boutet (eds) *France, pays multilingue*, vol. 2, Paris: L'Harmattan.

Dalbera-Stefanaggi, M.-J. (1991) 'Les Corses et leurs langues: science et conscience', in J.- C. Bouvier and C. Martel (eds) *Les Français et leurs langues*, Aix-en-Provence: Publications de l'Université de Provence.

Danner, M. (1993) 'Haiti on the Verge', *New York Review of Books*, 7 October 1993.

Darot, M. and Pauleau, C. (1993) 'Situation du français en Nouvelle-Calédonie', in D. de Robillard and M. Beniamino (eds), *Le Français dans l'espace francophone*, Paris: Champion.

Deniau, X. (1992) *La Francophonie* (2nd edn), Paris: Presses Universitaires de France.

Depecker, L. (1988) *Les Mots de la francophonie*, Paris: Belin.

Dictionnaire des termes officiels de la langue française (1994), Paris: Délégation générale à la langue française.

Dictionnaire féminin–masculin des professions, des titres et des fonctions (1991), Geneva: Métropolis.

Dumas, D. (1987) *Nos Façons de parler*, Sillery, Ontario: Presses de l'Université du Québec.

Duponchel, L. (1979) 'Le français en Côte d'Ivoire, au Dahomey et au Togo', in A. Valdman (ed.) *Le Français hors de France*, Paris: Champion.

Étiemble (1964) *Parlez-vous franglais?*, Paris: Gallimard.

Fallet, R. (1956) *La Grande Ceinture*, Paris: Denoël.

Fasold, R. (1984) *The Sociolinguistics of Society*, Oxford: Blackwell.

—— (1990) *The Sociolinguistics of Language*, Oxford: Blackwell.

de Féral, C. (1994) 'Appropriation du français dans le sud du Cameroun', *Langue française* 104: 37–48.

Fischer, M. (1987) *Sprachbewußtsein in Paris*, Vienna/Cologne/Graz: Böhlau.

Francard, M. (1990) *Ces Belges qui parlent français*, Louvain-la-Neuve: Université Catholique de Louvain.

Gadet, F. (1992) *Le Français populaire*, Paris: Presses Universitaires de France.

Gardner-Chloros, P. (1991) *Language Selection and Switching in Strasbourg*, Oxford: Clarendon Press.

Georgin, R. (1957) *Jeux de mots: de l'orthographe au style*, Paris: Bonne.

Giordan, H. (ed.) (1992) *Les Minorités en Europe: droits linguistiques et droits de l'homme*, Paris: Kimé.

Girard, E. and Kernel, B. (1994) *Ado/Parent le manuel: guide de conversation*, Paris: Hors Collection/Les Presses de la Cité.

Goosse, A. (1991) *La 'nouvelle' Orthographe: exposé et commentaires*, Paris/Louvain-la-Neuve: Duculot.

Gordon, D.C. (1978) *The French Language and National Identity*, The Hague: Mouton.

Grimm-Gobat, G. and Charpilloz, A. (1982) *La Romandie dominée*, Lausanne: Favre.

Guérivière, J. de la (1994) *Belgique: la revanche des langues*, Paris: Seuil.

Gueunier, N. (1991) 'La conscience linguistique en Touraine: marges et béoties', in J.-C. Bouvier and C. Martel (eds) *Les Français et leurs langues*, Aix-en-Provence: Publications de l'Université de Provence.

Guillou, M. (1993) *Francophonie: nouvel enjeu mondial*, Paris: Hatier.

Hauchecorne, F. (1996) 'L'accent du Havre: mythe ou réalité?', unpublished M.Phil. thesis, University of Southampton.

D'Hautel (1808) *Dictionnaire du bas-langage ou des manières de parler usités parmi le peuple*, Paris: D'Hautel.

Hélias, P.-J. (1975) *Le Cheval d'orgueil: mémoires d'un Breton du pays bigouden*, Paris: Plon.

Heredia, C. de (1983) 'Les parlers français des migrants' in APREF, *J'cause français, non?*, Paris: La Découverte/Maspero.

Hoche, C. 'Le double langage', *Les Cahiers de l'Express*, October 1994.

Holmes, J. (1992) *An Introduction to Sociolinguistics*, London: Longman.

Hoppe, D. (1976) *Aussprache und sozialer Status*, Kronberg: Scriptor.

Huyghes, F.-B. (1991) *La Langue de coton*, Paris: Laffont.

Kloss, H. and McConnell, G.D. (1984) *Linguistic Composition of the Nations of the World*, Quebec: Presses de l'Université Laval.

Kloss, H., McConnell, G.D. and Verdoodt, A. (1989) *Les Langues écrites du monde: relevé du degré et des modes d'utilisation*, Quebec: Presses de l'Université Laval.

Krop, P. (1995) *Tu fais l'avion par terre: dictionnaire franco-africain*, Paris: Lattès.

Lacoste-Dujardin, C. (1992) *Yasmina et les autres de Nanterre et d'ailleurs: filles de parents maghrébins en France*, Paris: La Découverte.

Lafage, S. (1988) '«Français façon là, y a pas son deux!» ou les chroniques de Moussa dans l'hebdomadaire *Ivoire-Dimanche*', *Humoresques: L'Humour d'expression française: actes du colloque international*, Paris 27–30 June 1988, 2: 175–80.

Lappin, K. (1982) 'Evaluation de la prononciation du français montréalais', *Revue québécoise de linguistique* 11: 93–111.

Le Maitre, N.-M.-T. (1994) 'Anglo-American Influence on the French Vocabulary', unpublished MA dissertation, University of Southampton.

Leeman-Bouix, D. (1994) *Les Fautes de français existent-elles?*, Paris: Seuil.

Léger, J.-M. (1987) *La Francophonie: grand dessein, grande ambiguïté*, Quebec: Hurtubise.

Lemoine, M. (1982) *Le Mal antillais: leurs ancêtres les Gaulois*, Paris: L'Harmattan.

Léopardini, J.-P. (1994) *Sauve qui peut la langue*, Paris: L'Archipel.

Lepoutre, D. (1994) 'Le langage, l'école et la rue', *Critiques sociales* 5: 5–12.

Lodge, R.A. (1993) *French: From Dialect to Standard*, London: Routledge.

McRae, K.D. (1983) *Conflict and Compromise in Multilingual Societies: Switzerland*, Waterloo, Ontario: Wilfrid Laurier University Press.

—— (1986) *Conflict and Compromise in Multilingual Societies: Belgium*, Waterloo, Ontario: Wilfrid Laurier University Press.

Mela, V. (1988) 'Parler verlan: règles et usage', *Langage et Société* 45: 47–72.

Merle, P. (1989) *Dictionnaire du français branché suivi du guide du français tic et toc*, Paris: Seuil.

—— (1991) *Le Déchiros*, Paris: Seuil.

Mougeon, R. (1994) 'Interventions gouvernementales en faveur du français au Québec et en Ontario', *Langage et Société* 67: 37–52.

Mougin, S. (1991) 'La conscience linguistique en Lorraine romane', in J.-C. Bouvier and C. Martel (eds) *Les Français et leurs langues*, Aix-en-Provence: Publications de l'Université de Provence.

Muller, B. (1985) *Le Français d'aujourd'hui*, Paris: Klincksieck.

Nève de Mévergnies, F.-X. (1984) '«Auquin doute: *un parfum brun* s'en va . . . ». La disparition du phonème /œ̃/ en français contemporain', *Le Français moderne* 52, 2: 198–219.

Ngalasso, M.M. (1988) 'Usages du français en milieu urbain africain', *Présence francophone* 33: 105–20.

—— (1994) 'Statut, usage et rôle du français au Zaïre', in S. Abou and K. Haddad (eds) *Une Francophonie différentielle*, Paris: L'Harmattan.

Offord, M. (1990) *Varieties of Contemporary French*, London: Macmillan.

—— (forthcoming) *French Sociolinguistics: A Reader*, Clevedon: Multilingual Matters.

Philippe, P.-A., Mamoud, M. and Tzanos, G.-O. (1996) *Le Dico de la banlieue*, Paris: La Sirène.

Picoche, J. and Marchello-Nizia, C. (1989) *Histoire de la langue française*, Paris: Nathan.

Pivot, B. (ed.) (1989) *Le Livre de l'orthographe*, Paris: Hatier.

Pohl, J. (1985) 'Le français de Belgique est-il belge?' *Présence francophone* 27: 9–19.

Pumain, D., Saint-Julien, T. and Ferras, R. (1990) *France, Europe du Sud*, Paris: Hachette/Reclus.

Rat, M. (1978) *Je connais mieux le français* (2nd edn), Verviers: Les Nouvelles Editions Marabout.

Richler, M. (1992) *Oh Canada! Oh Quebec! Requiem for a Divided Country*, London: Chatto & Windus.

de Robillard, D. and Beniamino, M. (eds) (1993) *Le Français dans l'espace francophone*, Vol. 1, Paris: Champion.

Rossillon, P. (1983) *Un milliard de Latins en l'an 2000?*, Paris: L'Harmattan.

—— (ed.) (1995) *Atlas de la langue française*, Paris: Bordas.

Sabatier, R. (1956) *Boulevard*, Paris: Albin Michel.

de Saint-Robert, P. (1986) *Lettre ouverte à ceux qui en perdent leur français*, Paris: Albin Michel.

San-Antonio (1974) *Un os dans la noce*, Paris: Fleuve Noir.

Sanders, C. (ed.) (1993) *French Today: Language in its Social Context*, Cambridge: Cambridge University Press.

Schifres, A. (1990) *Les Parisiens*, Paris: Lattès.

—— 'Euro z'élus', *L'Express*, 1 August 1991.

—— (1994) *Les Hexagons*, Paris: Laffont.

Schlaepfer, R., (1982) *La Suisse aux quatre langues*, Geneva: Éditions Zoë.

Schlieben-Lange, B. (1993) 'Occitan: French', in R. Posner and J.N. Green (eds) *Bilingualism and Linguistic Conflict in Romance*, Berlin: Mouton de Gruyter.

Seguin, B. and Teillard, F. (1996) *Les Céfrans parlent aux Français*, Paris: Calmann-Lévy.

Sempé-Goscinny (1960) *Le Petit Nicolas*, Paris: Denoël.

Simard, Y. (1994) 'Les français de Côte d'Ivoire', *Langue française* 104: 20–36.

Stevenson, P. (1995) *The German Language and the Real World*, Oxford: Clarendon.

Tabi Manga, J. (1990) 'Variation lexicale du français au Cameroun', in A. Clas and B. Ouoba (eds), *Visages du français: variétés lexicales de l'espace francophone*, Paris: John Libbey Eurotext.

Taverdet, G. (1990) 'Regionale Varianten des Französischen in Europa. I. Frankreich', in G. Holtus, M. Metzeltin and C. Schmitt (eds) *Lexikon der Romanistischen Linguistik*, vol. 5, Tübingen: Niemeyer.

Thiam, N. (1994) 'La variation sociolinguistique du code mixte wolof-français à Dakar: une première approche', *Langage et Société* 68: 11–34.

—— (1995) '«Un vrai Borain»: aspects sociolinguistiques du français parlé dans le Borinage', *Langage et Société* 74: 71–92.

Thiers, G. (1993) 'Language Contact and Corsican Polynomia', in R. Posner and J.N. Green (eds) *Bilingualism and Linguistic Conflict in Romance*, Berlin: Mouton de Gruyter.

Todd, L., (1990) *Pidgins and Creoles*, London: Routledge.

Tuaillon, G. (1988) 'Le Français régional; formes de rencontre', in G. Vermès (ed.) *Vingt-cinq communautés linguistiques de la France*, vol. 1, Paris: L'Harmattan.

Valdman, A. (1978) *Le Créole: structure, statut et origine*, Paris: Klincksieck.

—— (1979) *Le Français hors de France*, Paris: Champion.

Vandel, P. (1992) *Le Dico français/français: le livre-décodeur*, Paris: Lattès.

Walter, H. (1988) *Le Français dans tous les sens*, Paris: Laffont.

Wardhaugh, R. (1992) *An Introduction to Sociolinguistics*, Oxford: Blackwell.

Weber, E. (1979) *Peasants into Frenchmen: The Modernization of Rural France, 1870–1914*, London: Chatto & Windus.

Wexler, P.J. (1950) *La Formation du vocabulaire des chemins de fer en France (1778–1842)*, Geneva: Droz.

Index of terms
relating to language

(The number indicates the page on which the term is first introduced)